SWAHILI EXERCISES.

SO
LI
DEO
GL
OR
IA

LONDON:
GEORGE BELL AND SONS, YORK STREET,
COVENT GARDEN.
1882.

This scarce antiquarian book is included in our special *Legacy Reprint Series*. In the interest of creating a more extensive selection of rare historical book reprints, we have chosen to reproduce this title even though it may possibly have occasional imperfections such as missing and blurred pages, missing text, poor pictures, markings, dark backgrounds and other reproduction issues beyond our control. Because this work is culturally important, we have made it available as a part of our commitment to protecting, preserving and promoting the world's literature. Thank you for your understanding.

ADVERTISEMENT.

THIS little book is intended as a practical guide for those who wish to speak Swahili correctly. It does not pretend to teach them to speak the language, but to guide them to the use of correct forms, and to draw their attention to niceties of expression, which the untutored ear would probably miss. The only way to learn to speak a language is by listening to, and talking with, natives. Without this no book in the world can be of much use. But a listener will soon meet with forms and phrases which want explanation. It is then that he can make good use of a book. Thus a listener would soon find that the first syllables of Swahili words were often changing, but it would be very difficult for him without any guide to discover what rules the changes followed.

The first syllables of Swahili words depend almost always upon some Substantive expressed or understood. But if a learner is plunged at once into a chaos of ten or twelve or fifteen or sixteen different forms with various effects upon the other parts of speech, he is apt to give up the attempt to master what seems so much more difficult than it really is. In the following pages three of the most useful forms of Substantives are first taken, and by working through all the ordinary grammar of the language with these three forms only, the learner will find that his mind is getting used to the peculiarities of this class of languages, and the real simplicity of their construction will become more and more evident.

It is not intended to give instances here of every form of word or sentence. All the more important are given; what remain are rarely used, or belong to some specialty of thought or expression, and can be very soon mastered when they are really wanted. The compiler has been himself surprised to find how copious and expressive the Swahili language is, and he will be glad if these exercises help to vindicate its honour.

TABLE OF CONTENTS.

SUBSTANTIVES.
M- AND KI- CLASSES, 1—64.
List of regular Substantives, 1.
  Substantives with vowel roots, 24, 26.
Plurals, 1, 24, 26.
Possessive case, 28.
Locative case, 99.
Agreement of Adjectives, 3.
  Vowel Adjectives, 25.
  Numerals, 6.
Pronouns.
  Demonstratives, 7.
  Personal Pronouns, 10.
    Verbal Prefixes, 12.
  Interrogatives, 13.
  Objective prefixes, 21.
  Possessive Pronouns, 30.
  Him and His, 31.
  Quasi Pronouns, *all, having, itself, by itself,* 32.
  Relatives, 34.

THE N- CLASS, 79—91.
List of N- Substantives, 80.
Euphonic changes, 79, 88.
Adjectives, 85.
  Numerals, 86.
Pronouns, 87—90.
  Demonstratives, 88.
  Pronominal prefixes, 87, 91.

CONTENTS.

THE N- CLASS—*continued.*
    Which? 89.
    Possessives, 89.
    Quasi Pronouns, 89.
    Relatives, 90.

THE MA- CLASS, 67—91, *see* 110.
    List of Ma- Substantives, 68.
    Adjectives, 70.
    Pronouns, 72.
        Demonstratives, 72.
        Pronominal prefixes, 73—77.
        Which? 72.
        Possessives, 74.
        Quasi Pronouns, 75.
        Relatives, 76.

THE U- CLASS, 92—99.
    List of U- Substantives, 93.
    Plurals, 92.
    Adjectives, 96.
        Numerals, 96.
    Pronouns, 97.
        Demonstratives, 97.
        Pronominal prefixes, 97, 98.
        Which? 97.
        Relatives, 98.

MAHALI, place, 64.
INFINITIVES of Verbs as Substantives, 66.
NAMES OF ANIMALS, 110.
THE -NI CASE, 99.

ADJECTIVES.
    List of regular Adjectives, 4.
    List of vowel Adjectives, 25.

ADJECTIVES—*continued*.

    Indeclinable Adjectives, 101.
    Compound Adjectives, 103.
    Adjectival Verbs, 105.
    Comparison of Adjectives, 114.
    Agreement of Adjectives, 3, 25, 65, 66, 70, 85, 96, 103, 110.

NUMERALS, 6.

    Ordinal numbers, 104.
    Agreement of numerals, 6, 65, 66, 70, 86, 96, 110.

PRONOUNS.

    Demonstratives, 7, 65, 66, 72, 88, 97, 110.
    Personal Pronouns, 10.
    Subjective and Objective prefixes, 12, 21, 46, 65, 66, 73, 77, 87, 91, 97, 98, 110.
    Interrogatives, 13, 65, 72, 89, 97.
    Quasi Pronouns, *all, having, itself, by itself,* 32, 65, 66, 75, 89, 97.
    Possessive Pronouns, 30, 65, 66, 74, 89, 97.
    Relatives, 34—38, 116, 119, 124.
        Relative with negative, 52.
        Forming quasi Adjectives, 105.
        In the comparison of Adjectives, 106.
        Agreement of Relatives, 34, 66, 76, 90, 98.
        Relatives of time and place, 37, 66, 117, 119.
        Relative without note of time, 109.

THE VERB.

    List of Verbs, 16, 12.
    List of irregular Verbs, 121, 122.
    List of Adjectival Verbs, 106.
    Infinitive, 16, 66.

THE VERB—*continued.*

Indicative Tenses, affirmative.
  Present indefinite, 27.
  Present imperfect, 15, 35.
  Future, 15, 35.
  Future of continuing action, 126.
  Present Perfect, 12, 15, 105, 125.
  Past, 15, 28.
  Past Imperfect, 126.
  Pluperfect, 126.
  Narrative tense, 41.
  Participial tense, 43.
Indicative Negative, 46.
  Present, 47.
  Past, 48.
  Not yet Tense, 49.
  Future, 50.
  Negative with relatives, 52.
  Negative participial, 54.
Imperative affirmative, 38, 41.
  „ negative, 52.
Subjunctive affirmative, 38, 41.
  „ negative, 51.
Conditional affirmative, 45.
  „ negative, 51.
Compound tenses, 125.
  Kwisha, as an auxiliary, 126.
Participles, 125.

PASSIVE VOICE, 55, 127, 129, 131, 133.

TO BE, 115—120, 125, 126.
  See also 11, 14, 47, 53, 73, 87, 97, 114.

TO HAVE, 123—125.

DERIVATIVE VERBS, 127—135.
  Applied or Prepositional form, 127.

CONTENTS. xi

  With *mbali*, 132.
  To denote use or purpose, 131.
  Reciprocal form, 132.
  Reflexive, 22.
  Neuter form, 133.
  Causative form, 134.
  Verbs in -e, -i, and u-, 40, 47, 56, 130, 133, 135.
  Verbs in -oa and ua, 56, 129.

ADVERBS, 57.

  List of Adverbs, 57.
  Sana, 58, 114.
  Bado, 49.
  Mbali, 132.

PREPOSITIONS, 59.

  Prepositional form of Verb, 60, 127.
  Compound Prepositions, 60.
  Of, 28, 60, 65, 74, 89, 97, 103, 132.
  By after Passive Verb, 56.

CONJUNCTIONS, 61, 41, 43.

QUESTIONS, 13, 20, 37, 39.

ERRATUM.

"Nipitayo," p. 109, line 15, *should be* "Mpitayo."

PLURAL OF SUBSTANTIVES.

KI— AND M— CLASSES.

Substantives beginning with Ki- are made plural by changing Ki- into Vi-

 Kitu, *a thing.*   Vitu, *things.*

Substantives beginning with M- are made plural in different ways according to whether they are the names of persons, or living beings of any kind, or are the names of trees, or things in general.

If they denote living beings, substantives in M- are made plural by changing M- into Wa-

 Mtu, *a person.*   Watu, *people.*

If they do not denote living beings, substantives in M- are made plural by changing M- into Mi-

 Mti, *a tree, wood.*   Miti, *trees.*
 Mkono, *an arm.*   Mikono, *arms.*

What are the plurals of—

Kitendo, *an action.*   Kibofu, *a bladder.*
Mshale, *an arrow.*   Kipofu, *a blind person.*
Kikapo, *a matting bag.*   Mfupa, *a bone.*
Mbuyu, *a baobab tree.*   Kitabu, *a book.*
Kitanda, *a bedstead.*   Mpaka, *a boundary.*

Mzigo, *a burden.*
Kifungo, *a button.*
Mzinga, *a cannon.*
Mtumbwi, *a canoe.*
Msafara, *a caravan.*
Mkufu, *a chain.*
Kiti, *a chair.*
Mfalme, *a chief, a king.*
Mtoto, *a child.*
Kidevu, *the chin.*
Mnazi, *a cocoanut tree.*
Mbuni, *a coffee plant.*
Kitana, *a comb.*
Mpishi, *a cook.*
Kizibo, *a cork.*
Kikombe, *a cup.*
Mtende, *a date tree.*
Kiziwi, *a deaf person.*
Mlango, *a door.*
Mlevi, *a drunkard.*
Mzungu, *a European.*
Kidole, *a finger.*
Mvuvi, *a fisherman.*
Kiroboto, *a flea.*
Mguu, *the foot.*
Kivuko, *a ford.*
Mgeni, *a foreigner.*
Mchezo, *a game.*
Mlinzi, *a guard.*
Mkono, *the hand.*
Kipini, *a handle.*
Kitwa, *the head.*
Mchunga, *a herdsman.*
Kilima, *a hill.*
Kiboko, *hippopotamus.*
Kibanda, *a hut.*
Mkalimani, *an interpreter.*
Kisiwa, *an island.*
Kisu, *a knife.*
Kifuniko, *a lid.*
Mstari, *a line.*
Mdomo, *a lip.*
Mjusi, *a lizard.*
Mkate, *a loaf.*
Kioo, *a looking glass.*
Kitanzi, *a loop.*
Mchiro, *a mangouste.*
Mlingote, *a mast.*
Mganga, *a medicine-man.*
Msiba, *a misfortune.*
Kinu, *a wooden mortar for cleaning corn.*
Mlima, *a mountain.*
Kinwa, *the mouth.*
Mlezi, *a nurse.*
Kiapo, *an oath.*
Mzee, *an old person.*
Kitunguu, *an onion.*
Msimamizi, *an overlooker.*
Mchikichi, *a palm oil tree.*
Kipande, *a piece.*
Mto, *a pillow.*
Kipele, *a pimple.*
Mti, *a pole.*
Mpagazi, *a caravan porter.*
Kiazi, *a sweet potatoe.*

AGREEMENT OF ADJECTIVES. 3

Kigai, *a potsherd.*
Kifuko, *a purse.*
Kitambaa, *a rag.*
Kidaka, *a recess.*
Kifaru, *a rhinoceros.*
Mto, *a river.*
Mtoro, *a runaway.*
Mtai, *a scratch.*
Mtumishi, *a servant.*
Kivuli, *a shadow.*
Kiatu, *a shoe (sandal).*
Mgonjwa, *a sick person.*
Mjinga, *a simpleton.*
Mtumwa, *a slave.*
Mtwana, *a slave boy.*
Kijakazi, *a slave girl.*
Mjakazi, *a slave woman.*
Mjoli, *a fellow slave.*
Mkeka, *a sleeping mat.*
Kidonda, *a sore.*
Mkuke, *a spear.*
Mtambo, *a metal spring.*
Mkia, *a tail.*
Kijiko, *a teaspoon.*
Kiko, *a tobacco pipe.*
Mji, *a town.*
Mtego, *a trap.*
Kilemba, *a turban.*
Mzabibu, *a vine.*
Kisibau, *a waistcoat.*
Mtungi, *a waterjar.*
Kisima, *a well.*
Mjeledi, *a whip.*
Mke, *a wife.*
Mchawi, *a wizard.*
Kijana, *a youth.*

The English words are in alphabetical order.

MUUNGU, GOD, and *Mtume,* an Apostle, make their plurals irregularly, *miungu,* gods, *Mitume,* Apostles.

AGREEMENT OF ADJECTIVES.

Adjectives are made to agree with their substantives by adopting the same prefix.

Mtu mrefu, *a tall man.*
Watu warefu, *tall people.*
Miti mirefu, *tall trees.*
Kisu kirefu, *a long knife.*
Visu virefu, *long knives.*

AGREEMENT OF ADJECTIVES.

The Adjective is always placed after its substantive.

List of Adjectives,—the root only is here given, to which the proper prefix must be in each case attached.

Bad, —baya.
Bare, only, —tupu.
Beautiful, —zuri.
Bitter, —chungu.
Broad, —pana.
Chief, great, —kuu.
Dry, —kavu.
Empty, —tupu.
Female, —ke.
Fierce, —kali.
Fine, —zuri.
Foreign, —geni.
Great, large, —kubwa.
Hard, —gumu.
Heavy, —zito.
Idle, —vivu.
Jealous, —wivu.
Little, —dogo.
Long, —refu.
New, —pya.
Old (worn out), —kukuu.
Open, —wazi.
Raw, —bichi.
Ripe, —bivu.
Rotten, —bovu.
Savage, —kali.
Sharp, —kali.
Short, —fupi.
Sound, —zima.
Sweet, —tamu.
Thick, —nene.
Unripe, —bichi.
Whole, —zima.
Wide, —pana.

The interrogative *How many?* -ngapi? is treated as an adjective.

Watu wangapi? *How many people?*
Viti vingapi? *How many chairs?*
Miti mingapi? *How many trees?*

Translate into Swahili.

A bad action. A long arrow. Empty matting bags. Thick baobab trees. A broad bedstead.

AGREEMENT OF ADJECTIVES.

A hard bone. An old book. Heavy burdens. A beautiful button. Large cannons. A short canoe. Foreign caravans. A thick chain. A new chair. Great chiefs. A beautiful child. Long chins. A fine coffee plant. Little combs. An idle cook. Hard corks. An empty cup. Short date trees. Wide doors. A fierce drunkard. Female Europeans. A thick finger. Jealous fishermen. Bare feet. A wide ford. Idle foreigners. A fine game. Fierce guards. A sound hand. Long handles. A dry head. Bad herdsmen. A great hill. A dry hut. A bad interpreter. Large islands. A sharp knife. Heavy lids. A long line. Dry lips. Large lizards. A sweet loaf. New lookingglasses. A long loop. Female mangoustes. A short mast. A foreign medicine man. Heavy misfortunes. A new mortar. Great mountains. Wide mouths. Jealous nurses. A bitter oath. Fine old people. A rotten onion. Sharp overlookers. Little palm oil trees. Short pieces. A hard pillow. Long poles. An idle porter. Raw sweet potatoes. A sharp potsherd. Empty purses. An old rag. Wide recesses. Foreign simpletons. A new slave. Idle slave women. Bad slave boys. A jealous fellow-slave. Open sores. A heavy spear. Wide rivers. A new shoe. Bad servants. A long shadow. Old sleeping mats. A small tea-spoon. Long tails. A short tobacco pipe. Large towns. An empty trap. Beautiful turbans. A fine vine. Long waistcoats. An empty water jar. Heavy whips. A jealous wife. Large unripe sweet potatoes. How many burdens? How many huts? How many loaves? How many cooks? How many mountains? How many simpletons? How many towns? How many pieces?

How many water jars? How many knives?

NUMBERS.

The Swahili numbers are treated as adjectives, and made to agree with their substantives in the same way.

The words for six, seven, nine, and ten, are irregular, being used without any prefix.

The root forms of the numbers are

1 —moja.	7 Saba.
2 —wili.	8 —nane.
3 —tatu.	9 Kenda, *or* Tissa,
4 —nne.	*or* Tissia.
5 —tano.	10 Kumi.
6 Sita.	

Mtu mmoja, *one man.*
Kitu kimoja, *one thing.*
Miti mitatu, *three trees.*
Vitu vinne, *four things.*
Watu wanane, *eight people.*
Miti sita, *six trees.*
Vitu kenda, *nine things.*
Watu kumi, *ten men.*

Where an adjective is joined with the substantive as well as a numeral, they are usually placed in exactly the reverse of the English order.

Watu wabaya wawili, *two bad men.*
Miti mizuri mitatu, *three fine trees.*

Translate into Swahili.

One man. One turban. One knife. One tree. One purse. One slave. One river. One water jar. Two burdens. Three buttons. Four cannons. Five canoes. Six caravans. Seven chains. Eight chairs. Nine chiefs. Ten children. One small cocoanut tree. Two large coffee plants. Three long combs. Four idle cooks. Five bad corks. Six small cups. Seven large date trees. Nine wide doors. Ten short Europeans. One thick finger. Three broad feet. Four long handles. Five great hills. Seven new huts. Eight bad interpreters. Nine sharp knives. Ten long lines. One savage mangouste.

THIS and THAT.

The two demonstratives in Swahili answering to THIS and THAT denote strictly what is near and what is at a distance. Where THIS and THAT are used in English to distinguish two things which are both near, the same word must be used for both in Swahili. The second demonstrative answers to YONDER, or very closely to the north of England word YON.

All the demonstratives pointing to things near begin with *h-*, and all those pointing to things at a distance end with *-le*.

Mtu huyu, *this man.*
Mtu yule, *that man.*
Watu hawa, *these men.*
Watu wale, *those men.*

DEMONSTRATIVES.

Mti huu, *this tree*.
Mti ule, *that tree*.
Miti hii, *these trees*.
Miti ile, *those trees*.
Kitu hiki, *this thing*.
Kitu kile, *that thing*.
Vitu hivi, *these things*.
Vitu vile, *those things*.

The second syllable of the demonstrative THIS is the first of the demonstrative THAT. Particular care must be taken to remember this syllable, as it is the foundation of all the forms of Pronouns.

In nouns of the *Mtu* class, it is -*yu*- in the singular and -*wa*- in the plural.
In nouns of the *Mti* class, it is -*u*- in the singular and -*i*- in the plural.
In nouns of the *Ki*- class, it is -*ki*- in the singular and -*vi*- in the plural.

The demonstrative THIS is made by prefixing *h* and the root vowel, *h-u-yu, h-a-wa, h-u-u, h-i-i, h-i-ki, h-i-vi*.

The demonstrative THAT or YONDER is made by adding -*le, yu-le, wa-le, u-le, i-le, ki-le, vi-le*.

If an adjective is joined with the substantive the demonstrative follows both.

Mtu mbaya huyu, *this bad man*.
Miti mibovu hii, *these rotten trees*.
Vitu vidogo hivi, *these little things*.

DEMONSTRATIVES.

Translate into Swahili.

This fine action. Yonder long arrows. This thick baobab tree. Those bedsteads. This bladder. These hard bones. This large book. This boundary. Yonder heavy burdens. These buttons. Those large cannons. This caravan. These chains. Yonder chair. Those chiefs. These children. This cocoanut tree. That coffee plant. These combs. This cook. This cork. Yonder cup. Yonder date tree. These doors. This drunkard. These Europeans. This finger. Those fishermen. Those feet. This foot. This ford. This foreigner. These games. These guards. These hands. These handles. That herdsman. This little hill. Those small huts. Those interpreters. Those large islands. That long knife. This lid. These thick lines. These thick lips. Those beautiful lizards. Those sweet loaves. That tall mast. That great mountain. These old people. Those raw onions. This pimple. That pole. Those idle porters. These small sweet potatoes. That sharp potsherd. Those old rags. That simpleton. These idle slaves. That short heavy spear. That old shoe. These servants. Those new sleeping mats. This tobacco pipe. These traps. Those fine turbans. These fine waistcoats. These new waterjars. This well. These wizards.

When the demonstrative precedes the adjective, it must be very often translated by the introduction, in the English, of the verb *to be*.

Miti hii mirefu, *these poles are long.*
Kisu hiki kikali, *this knife is sharp.*
Mtu huyu mbaya, *this man is bad.*

Translate into Swahili.

These people are fierce. These mountains are large. These slaves are idle. Yonder trees are small. That man is short. This spear is heavy. These Europeans are jealous.

PERSONAL PRONOUNS.

The full forms of the personal pronouns in Swahili are

    Mimi, *I.*   Sisi, *we.*
    Wewe, *thou* or *you.* Ninyi, *you.*
    Yeye, *he* or *she.* Wao, *they.*

These forms can refer only to persons or living beings. For things the demonstrative pronouns are used.

The second person is always used in the singular when one person only is addressed.

When a pronoun is followed by an adjective it implies the appropriate form of the verb *to be.*

    Mimi mkubwa, *I am great.*
    Wewe mdogo, *you are small.*
    Hii mitamu, *they* (these) *are sweet.*
    Ile mirefu, *they* (those) *are tall.*

In order to agree with the plural personal pronouns *sisi, ninyi,* and *wao,* adjectives prefix *wa-* as if to agree with *watu.*

Translate into Swahili.

  *** The words in parentheses are not to be translated.

I am fierce. You are short. He is large. They

PERSONAL PRONOUNS. 11

are small. We are heavy. You (pl.) are dry. They (shoes) are new. It (rag) is old. They (huts) are old. It (chain) is thick. They (slaves) are idle. They (sweet potatoes) are ripe. He is little. He is savage. She is foreign. I am jealous. You (pl.) are jealous. They (people) are beautiful. It (waterjar) is empty. He is short. You are large. You (pl.) are large.

The personal pronouns are generally represented by a prefix attached to the verb. These prefixes may be used alone to express the present tense of the verb *to be*.

They are the same as the second syllable of the demonstrative *this* (see p. 8).

    Ni, *I am.*   Tu, *we are.*
    U, *you are.*   'M, *you are.*
    Yu, *he or she is.*   Wa, *they are.*
    U or Ki, *it is.*   I or Vi, *they are.*

The full forms of the personal pronouns may be used to give particular emphasis.

    Mimi ni mzuri, *as for me I am beautiful.*
    Wewe u mvivu, *you at all events are idle.*

Translate into Swahili.

This tree is little. That date tree is short. This old man is great. We are dry. Those poles are long. That little man is fierce. That knife is sharp. You are idle. He is idle. He is little. She is beautiful. She is short. It (the knife) is heavy. It (the knife) is long. It (the sweet potatoe) is raw. They (the sweet potatoes) are ripe. They (the old people) are beautiful. You are short. It (the hut) is old. They (the rags) are old. They (the rags) are new. They (the huts) are new. They (the poles) are rotten. It (the book) is new.

The persons of the verb are denoted by prefixes differing from those given above only in the third person singular, which when referring to living beings is denoted by *a-*, whatever the form of the substantive may be.

Yu- is employed in other dialects, but scarcely ever in that of Zanzibar.

Thus the present perfect of the verb *to love* is expressed by —*mependa* with the proper personal prefix.

   Nimependa, *I have loved.*
   Umependa, *you have loved.*
   Amependa, *he or she has loved.*
 Kimependa, *or* Umependa, *it has loved.*
   Tumependa, *we have loved.*
   Mmependa, *you have loved.*
   Wamependa, *they have loved.*
 Vimependa *or* Imependa, *they have loved*

** -mependa, *has loved;* -meanguka, *has fallen;* -mevunjika, *is broken;* -mekufa, *has died* or *is dead;* -meonekana, *has become visible* or *is in sight;* -mepasuka, *is split.*

Translate into Swahili.

That arrow is broken. The matting bag has fallen. The baobab tree has fallen. That old bedstead is broken. The old person is dead. The large bone is broken. The new book is split. The boundary is visible. The heavy burden has fallen. The buttons are broken. The canoes are visible. The large caravan is in sight. The thick chains are broken. The chain has fallen. The great chiefs are dead. The little child is dead. That tall cocoa-nut tree has fallen. The old water jar is broken. The little comb is broken. The cook is in sight. The cup is broken. These new cups are broken. Two date trees are fallen. Four doors are broken. That drunkard has fallen. Seven Europeans are dead. Two fingers are broken.

INTERROGATIVES.

There are five interrogatives which do not vary.

    Nani? *Who?*
    Lini? *When?*
    Nini? *What?*
    Gani? *Of what sort?*
    Wapi? *Where?*

The interrogative *Which?* is formed by adding -pi to the pronominal syllable.

    Mtu yupi? *Which man?*
    Watu wapi? *Which people?*
    Mti upi? *Which tree?*
    Miti ipi? *Which trees?*
    Kitu kipi? *Which thing?*
    Vitu vipi? *Which things?*

Where the substantive is not expressed, the interrogative must be in form proper to the substantive which is understood.

    Upi? *Which?* (tree)
    Yupi? *Which?* (man)
    Vipi? *Which?* (things)

INTERROGATIVES.

The interrogatives *lini, gani,* and *wapi* always follow the words they are connected with.

 Amekuja lini? *When did he come?*
 Mti gani? *What sort of tree?*

If followed by a demonstrative the verb *to be* is implied.

 Vitu gani hivi? *What sort of things are these?*
 Nani huyu? *Who is this?*
 Nani mzee huyu? *Who is this old man?*
 Nini hii? *What are these?*

Translate into Swahili.

What sort of people are these? Which arrows? What sort of matting bags? Which baobab tree? What sort of a bedstead is this? Who is this old person? What sort of bone is this? Which books? What sort of buttons? Which canoe? What sort of a chain? Which chair? What sort of chiefs are these? Which child? Which cocoanut trees? Which date tree? Who is this drunkard? What sort of a chief is this drunkard? What sort of trees are those? Which hand? What sort of game is this? Which hill? Which islands are those? What sort of thing is this knife? What sort of man [i.e. of what tribe] is this interpreter? Which mast? What sort of misfortune? What (sort of) mountains are those? What sort of tree is a palm oil tree? What is an oath? What sort of an overlooker is a blind person? Which old person is the deaf man? Which (man) is the medicine man? What sort of pole? Which poles?

THE VERB.

The verb is conjugated by the use of tense prefixes and personal prefixes. The personal prefixes are those given above. The following are some of the tense prefixes.

PRESENT IMPERFECT, -na-

PRESENT PERFECT, -me-

PAST PERFECT, -li-

FUTURE, -ta-

Ninapenda, *I am loving.*
Nimependa, *I have loved.*
Nilipenda, *I loved.*
Nitapenda, *I shall love.*

Unapenda, *you are loving.*
Umependa, *you have loved.*
Ulipenda, *You loved.*
Utapenda, *You will love.*

Anapenda, *He or she is loving.*
Amependa, *He has loved.*
Alipenda, *He loved.*
Atapenda, *He will love.*

Unaanguka, *It* [nti] *is falling.*
Umeanguka, *It has fallen.*
Ulianguka, *It fell.*
Utaanguka, *It will fall.*

Kinaanguka, *It* [kitu] *is falling.*
Kimeanguka, *It has fallen.*
Kilianguka, *It fell.*
Kitaanguka, *It will fall.*

Tunapenda, *We are loving.*
Tumependa, *We have loved.*
Tulipenda, *We loved.*
Tutapenda, *We shall love.*
Mnapenda, *You are loving.*
Mmependa, *You have loved.*
Mlipenda, *You loved.*
Mtapenda, *You will love.*
Wanapenda, *They [watu] are loving.*
Wamependa, *They have loved.*
Walipenda, *They loved.*
Watapenda, *They will love.*
Inaanguka, *They [miti] are falling.*
Imeanguka, *They have fallen.*
Ilianguka, *They fell.*
Itaanguka, *They will fall.*
Vinaanguka, *They [vitu] are falling.*
Vimeanguka, *They have fallen.*
Vilianguka, *They fell.*
Vitaanguka, *They will fall.*

The infinitive is made by prefixing *ku-*

List of Verbs.

Kukubali, *to accept.*
 ,, shtaki, *to accuse.*
 ,, patana, *to agree.*
 ,, badili, *to alter.*
 ,, sumbua, *to annoy.*
 ,, jibu, *to answer.*
 ,, fika, *to arrive, to reach.*
 ,, uliza, *to ask.*
 ,, amka, *to awake.*
 ,, oga, *to bathe.*

Kuzaa, *to bear fruit.*
 ,, piga, *to beat.*
 ,, omba, *to beg.*
 ,, sadiki, *to believe.*
 ,, uma, *to bite.*
 ,, vuma, *to blow.*
 ,, jisifu, *to boast.*
 ,, chemka, *to boil.*
 ,, zaliwa, *to be born.*
 ,, piga kofi, *to box the ears.*

VERBS.

Kuvunja, *to break.*
„ leta, *to bring.*
„ jenga, *to build.*
„ waka, *to burn* (neut.).
„ teketeza, *to burn* (act.).
„ zika, *to bury.*
„ nunua, *to buy.*
„ ita, *to call.*
„ angalia, *to take care.*
„ tunza, *to take care of.*
„ chukua, *to carry.*
„ pakia, *to carry as cargo.*
„ kamata, *to catch hold of.*
„ daka, *to catch in the hand.*
„ geuka, *to be changed.*
„ danganya, *to cheat.*
„ tafuna, *to chew.*
„ chagua, *to choose.*
„ piga makofi, *to clap the hands.*
„ safisha, *to clean.*
„ panda, *to climb up.*
„ kusanya, *to collect.*
„ rudi, *to come back.*
„ karibia, *to come near to.*
„ toka, *to come, or go out.*
„ shinda, *to conquer.*
„ fikiri, *to consider.*
„ pika, *to cook.*
„ kohoa, *to cough.*
„ funika, *to cover.*
„ vuka, *to cross over.*
„ seta, *to crush.*

Kulia, *to cry.*
„ lima, *to cultivate.*
„ ponya, *to cure.*
„ kata, *to cut, to cut down.*
„ cheza, *to dance.*
„ pungua, *to decrease.*
„ linda, *to defend.*
„ kawia, *to delay.*
„ kana, *to deny.*
„ haribu, *to destroy.*
„ chimba, *to dig.*
„ agiza, *to direct.*
„ gawanya, *to divide.*
„ fanya, *to do.*
„ kokota, *to drag.*
„ vuta, *to draw.*
„ piga mstari, *to draw a line.*
„ teka maji, *to draw water.*
„ ota, *to dream.*
„ fukuza, *to drive away.*
„ kauka, *to get dry.*
„ anika, *to put out to dry.*
„ mwaga, *to empty out.*
„ isha, *to end.*
„ ingia, *to enter.*
„ okoka, *to escape.*
„ eleza, *to explain.*
„ punguka, *to fail.*
„ anguka, *to fall.*
„ funga, *to fasten, bind, shut.*
„ ogopa, *to fear.*

c

VERBS.

Kulisha, *to feed.*
„ pigana, *to fight.*
„ ona, *to find.*
„ maliza, *to finish.*
„ isha, *to be finished.*
„ kaza, *to fix.*
„ ruka, *to fly.*
„ kunja, *to fold.*
„ fuata, *to follow.*
„ gombeza, *to forbid.*
„ sahau, *to forget.*
„ samehe, *to forgive.*
„ pata, *to get.*
„ lewa, *to get drunk.*
„ toka, *to get out.*
„ ondoka, *to get up.*
„ rudi, *to go back.*
„ oza, *to go bad.*
„ tangulia, *to go before.*
„ pita, *to go by.*
„ shuka, *to go, or come down.*
„ saga, *to grind.*
„ linda, *to guard.*
„ thuru, *to harm.*
„ chukia, *to hate.*
„ sikia, *to hear.*
„ sayidia, *to help.*
„ ficha, *to hide.*
„ zuia, *to hinder.*
„ tweka, *to hoist.*
„ shika, *to hold.*
„ uma, *to hurt.*
„ unga, *to join.*
„ amua, *to judge.*
„ ruka, *to jump.*

Kupiga teke, *to kick.*
„ ua, *to kill.*
„ chinja, *to kill for food.*
„ jua, *to know.*
„ cheka, *to laugh.*
„ jifunza, *to learn.*
„ acha, *to leave.*
„ aga, *to take leave of.*
„ inua, *to lift up.*
„ penda, *to like.*
„ sikiliza, *to listen.*
„ tazama, *to look.*
„ tafuta, *to look for.*
„ legeza, *to loosen.*
„ potea, *to be lost.*
„ penda, *to love.*
„ shusha, *to lower.*
„ fanya, *to make.*
„ oa, *to marry a wife.*
„ pima, *to measure.*
„ onana, *to meet.*
„ kuta, *to meet with.*
„ yeyuka, *to melt.*
„ kosa, *to miss.*
„ changanya, *to mix.*
„ amuru, *to order.*
„ pindua, *to overturn.*
„ wiwa, *to owe.*
„ uma, *to pain.*
„ pita, *to pass.*
„ lipa, *to pay.*
„ okota, *to pick up.*
„ weka, *to place.*
„ pendeza, *to please.*
„ mimina, *to pour.*
„ sifu, *to praise.*

VERBS.

Kuomba, *to pray.*
  „ fanikiwa, *to prosper.*
  „ vuta, *to pull.*
  „ ng'oa, *to pull up.*
  „ sukuma, *to push.*
  „ tia, *to put.*
  „ weka, *to put away.*
  „ vaa, *to put on (clothes).*
  „ toa, *to put out.*
  „ zima, *to put out a light.*
  „ gombana, *to quarrel.*
  „ soma, *to read.*
  „ pokea, *to receive.*
  „ kumbuka, *to recollect.*
  „ kataa, *to refuse.*
  „ juta, *to regret.*
  „ furahi, *to rejoice.*
  „ salia, *to remain over.*
  „ kaa, *to remain (in a place).*
  „ kumbuka, *to remember.*
  „ kumbusha, *to remind.*
  „ pumzika, *to rest.*
  „ rudi, *to return, to go back.*
  „ rudisha, *to return, to give back.*
  „ oka, *to roast.*
  „ oza, *to rot.*
  „ viringa, *to be round.*
  „ sugua, *to rub.*
  „ piga mbio, *to run.*
  „ kimbia, *to run away, to flee.*
  „ sema, *to say.*

Kutawanya, *to scatter.*
  „ tharau, *to scorn.*
  „ kuna, *to scratch.*
  „ tafuta, *to search for.*
  „ ona, *to see.*
  „ peleka, *to send.*
  „ shona, *to sew.*
  „ tikisa, *to shake.*
  „ nyoa, *to shave.*
  „ onyesha, *to show.*
  „ imba, *to sing.*
  „ zama, *to sink.*
  „ kaa kitako, *to sit down.*
  „ lala, *to sleep.*
  „ nuka, *to smell* (n.)
  „ sikitika, *to be sorry.*
  „ nena, *to speak.*
  „ tumia, *to spend.*
  „ mwaga, *to spill.*
  „ pasua, *to split.*
  „ enea, *to spread* (n.)
  „ simama, *to stand.*
  „ kaa, *to stay.*
  „ piga, *to strike.*
  „ tosha, *to suffice.*
  „ toshea, *to surprise.*
  „ zunguka, *to surround.*
  „ fagia, *to sweep.*
  „ vimba, *to swell.*
  „ twaa, *to take.*
  „ angalia, *to take care.*
  „ vua, *to take off clothes.*
  „ sema, *to talk.*
  „ onja, *to taste.*
  „ fundisha, *to teach.*

VERBS.

Kutatua, *to tear (cloth, &c.)*. Kugeuka, *to turn* (neut.).
„ rarua, *to tear in pieces.* „ funua, *to uncover.*
„ ambia, *to tell.* „ fungua, *to unfasten, open.*
„ fikiri, *to think, to consider.*
„ thani, *to think, to suppose.* „ tumia, *to use.*
„ ngoja, *to wait.*
„ tembea, *to walk.*
„ tupa, *to throw.* „ taka, *to want.*
„ funga, *to tie.* „ osha, *to wash.*
„ choka, *to become tired.* „ futa, *to wipe.*
„ gusa, *to touch.* „ nyima, *to withhold.*
„ safiri, *to travel.* „ taajabu, *to wonder.*
„ jaribu, *to try.* „ abudu, *to worship.*
„ geuza, *to turn* (act.). „ andika, *to write.*

⁎ In Swahili a *question* is written in the same form as an *assertion*.

Umesikia. *You have heard.*
Umesikia? *Have you heard?*

Translate into Swahili.

I have accepted. Thou wilt accuse. We have agreed. They (things) will alter. They (people) will annoy. I answered. They (trees) are bearing fruit. The blind man is begging. I believe. The chiefs have arrived. The simpletons are asking. The hippopotamus is awaking. We shall bathe. The fleas will bite. The children are boasting. Four children have been born. The Europeans have bought. The cook built. You (pl.) bought. The old people called. She is taking care. The caravan porters are carrying. The overseer caught in his hand. The date tree is changed. The medicine men have cheated. The chief will choose. The herdsmen are clapping their hands. The child will climb up. The European will conquer. I am con-

VERBS. 21

sidering. The cook has cooked. They are coughing. The lid covered. That caravan has crossed over. These children will cry. The slaves will cultivate. Those sharp knives will cut. The slave women are dancing. Misfortunes are decreasing. Those bad slaves are delaying. The slave boys dug. We shall divide. He has done. Those slaves have drawn water. I have drawn a line. That old man dreamed. The onion has got dry. The drunkards are fighting. The arrow entered. The tall trees fell. The six Europeans have got drunk. The loaf has gone bad. The women slaves are grinding. The chief went before. You listened. You will cook. I am looking for. The old man has married a wife. That piece has melted. They will pay. We picked up. The savage chief prospered. You (sing.) are pushing. I am reading. The chief refused. The slave regretted. The caravan porters are resting. That hand is swelling.

THE OBJECTIVE PREFIX.

When the object of the verb is some definite thing it is denoted by a prefix inserted after the tense prefix. The objective prefix is generally the same as the subjective or personal prefix. It differs only in the second, and in the third persons when referring to persons or animated beings.

Me, —ni—   *Us,* —tu—
Thee, —ku—   *You,* —wa—
Him or *her,* —m— *Them,* —wa—
It (mti), —u—   *Them* (mti), —i—
It (kitu), —ki—   *Them* (vitu), —vi—

Ananipenda, *he likes me.*
Anakupenda, *he likes you.*

VERBS.

Anampenda, *he likes him* or *her*.
Anaupenda, *he likes it (the tree)*.
Anakipenda, *he likes it (the thing)*.
Anatupenda, *he likes us*.
Anawapenda, *he likes you* (pl.).
Anawapenda, *he likes them (people)*.
Anaipenda, *he likes them (the trees)*.
Anavipenda, *he likes them (the things)*.

Substantives and pronouns have no distinct form for the accusative or objective case.

Mtu anapiga mtu, *a man is beating a man*.

When the object of the verb is expressed and the objective prefix is also employed, the definite article must ordinarily be used in the English.

Anapiga mtu, *he is beating a man*.
Anampiga mtu, *he is beating the man*.
Anakata mti, *he is cutting down a tree*.
Anaukata mti, *he is cutting down the tree*.

When the object of the verb is expressed by a pronoun the objective prefix must always be used.

Anampiga, *he is beating him*.
Anampiga yule, *he is beating that man*.
Anaukata, *he is cutting it down (the tree)*.
Anaukata ule, *he is cutting down that tree*.

-self is denoted by -ji-.

Najipenda, *I love myself*.
Utajiuma, *you will hurt yourself*.
Amejificha, *he has hidden himself*.

Translate into Swahili.

This action annoys me. The arrow hit him. Those arrows missed them. He is carrying six matting

VERBS.

bags. Three baobab trees have fallen. They have brought two bedsteads. They have brought the two bedsteads. You will leave the bones. I have seen the book. They have passed the boundaries. Six caravan porters are carrying the nine burdens. You are unfastening the button. Ten men are dragging the two large cannons. Six men pushed the canoe. I see a caravan. You saw the two caravans. He will fasten the chain. The chief has brought a chair. I shall get that chair. The chiefs will pay me. I met with four children. You have passed the children. The Europeans have cut down the cocoanut trees. The cook has broken this waterjar. The slave girl has got a beautiful comb. The herdsman is beating the cook. I want a cook. I have cut the cork. He has picked up a cup. Those two date trees are bearing fruit. The door has rotted. The Europeans have killed that idle cook. This finger is paining me. The ten fishermen are coming back. I have killed seven fleas. The handle struck the foot. They saw the foreigners. The guards ran away. They lifted up two hands. We saw the hands. We passed two hills. The Europeans killed six hippopotamus. The strangers built two huts. The chief burnt down the two huts. The little interpreter boasted. The interpreter showed me [the] two large islands. You have received the knife. The cook is rubbing the lid. He showed me [the] line. The foreigner has cut the loaf. I have broken the looking glasses. The two masts are broken. I have found the little mountain. The nurse is feeding the children. The old people are listening. I have tasted the onions. The overseer is beating the slaves. I am looking for a palm oil tree. The mangouste has bitten that piece. The slave will bring a pillow. The poles have arrived.

I will pay the caravan porters. The sweet potatoes have gone bad. They will crush the potsherds. He brought the empty purse. We tore the rag. I saw six recesses. The slaves loved themselves. The chief is praising himself. You have tied yourself. The children fed themselves. They will harm themselves. The simpletons are overturning themselves. The idle slaves are scratching themselves.

VOWEL ROOTS.

I. The *m* prefix, however employed, appears generally before a vowel root as *mw*; the *w* is very faint before *o* and *u*, and often seems entirely to disappear.

The *wa*— prefix coalesces with an initial *e* or *i* into the sound of *we*—.

Substantives in M- followed by a vowel, with their plurals.

    Mwaka, *a year.* (miaka)
    Mwalimu, *a teacher.* (waalimu)
    Mwamba, *a rock.* (miamba)
    Mwamuzi, *a judge.* (waamuzi)
    Mwana, *a son.* (waana)
    Mwandishi, *a writer.* (waandishi)
    Mwanzo, *a beginning.* (mianzo)
    Mwashi, *a mason.* (waashi)
    Mwana mume, *a man.* (waana waume)
    Mwana mke, *a woman.* (waana wake)
    Mwavuli, *an umbrella.* (miavuli)
    Mwembe, *a mango tree.* (miembe)
    Mwenyewe, *the owner.* (wenyewe)
    Mwenzi, *a companion.* (wenzi)
    Mwezi, *the moon, or a month.* (miezi)
    Mwiba, *a thorn.* (miiba)

VOWEL ROOTS.

Mwiko, *a spoon.* (miiko)
Mwili, *the body.* (miili)
Mwisho, *the end.* (miisho)
Mwivi, *a thief.* (wevi)
Mwoga, *a coward.* (waoga)
Mwokozi, *a saviour.* (waokozi)
Moshi, *smoke.* (mioshi)
Moto, *fire.* (mioto)
Moyo, *the heart.* (mioyo)

Adjectives beginning with a vowel.

Black, —eusi.
Cunning, —erevu.
Different, —ingine.
Easy, —epesi.
Gentle, —anana.
Good, —ema.
Having, —enyi.
Light (not dark), —eupe.
Light (not heavy), —epesi.
Male, —ume.
Many, much, —ingi.
Narrow, —embamba.
Other, —ingine.
Red, —ekundu.
Slender, —embamba.
Soft, —ororo.
White, eupe.

Translate into Swahili.

I saw four red people. Two black people found a white person. This line is narrow. I drew a black line. The fire is burning. These burdens are light. Those black burdens are heavy. A light heart. Thick (zito) smoke. We shall see the black smoke. We shall leave two large fires. You have forgotten those hearts. Those years are short. Two teachers taught me. The white rock has sunk. I have told the judge. The four judges heard us. You will call the writer. I heard the bad beginning. Two good beginnings. The two masons built two huts. This mason used many poles. The Europeans bought many large umbrellas. They are cutting down those good mango trees. We have passed the owners. The beautiful moon has sunk. These months are good, those are bad. Two thorns entered the hand. These spoons are large [and] beautiful. The thieves ran away. Two cunning thieves took the canoe. The cowards feared the old man.

II. The *ki-* and *vi-* prefixes before a vowel become *ch-* and *vy-*.

    Kitu chekundu, *a red thing.*
    Vitu vyekundu, *red things.*
    Chombo kikubwa, *a large vessel.*
    Kitu cheusi kimoja, *one black thing.*
    Vitu vyeusi viwili, *two black things.*
Chombo kidogo kizuri, *a beautiful little vessel.*

Substantives of the ki- class in which the prefix becomes ch- because followed by a vowel.

    Chakula, *food.* (vyakula)
    Chambo, *a bait.* (vyambo)
    Chango, *a peg.* (vyango)
    Chanu, *a wooden platter used for carrying mortar.* (vyanu)
    Cheo, *measurement.* (vyeo)
    Cheti, *a passport.* (vyeti)
    Chombo, *a vessel.* (vyombo)
    Choo, *a watercloset.* (vyoo)
    Chura, *a frog.* (vyura)
    Chuma, *iron, or a piece of iron* (vyuma)
    Chumba, *a chamber, a room.* (vyumba)
    Chungu, *an earthen cooking pot.* (vyungu)
    Chuo, *a book.* (vyuo)
    Chusa, *a harpoon.* (vyusa)

Slaves and others from the interior often incorrectly change the ki- prefix into chi-, after the analogy of the Yao and other inland languages. Thus they say chikapo, *a basket*, for kikapu, chidogo, *little*, for kidogo, chilezo, *a buoy*, for kilezo, and so forth. In correct Swahili ki- never becomes chi-, but only ch- before a vowel.

Translate into Swahili.

Good food. The fisherman has taken the bait. These five black pegs. I have bought ten large mortar platters. This measurement is short. I have got two passports. He saw one red vessel. I have seen six black vessels. Ten cunning frogs. Iron is heavy. These irons are light. You have brought one red cooking pot. I shall want three small black cooking pots. You will carry that large book. He is carrying two thick red books. I took the large harpoon.

VOWEL TENSES.

The Indefinite Present is denoted by the prefix -a-. The Past Perfect is often formed by the prefix -ali-.

Before the vowel the personal prefixes become, n-[I], w-[you], tw-[we], mw-[you], w-[they], w- or ch-[it], y- or vy-[they].

The a- which is the sign of the third person singular is absorbed into the -a- of the tense prefix and disappears. The -a- of the plural prefix wa- disappears in the same manner.

THE POSSESSIVE CASE.

Nataka, *I want.*
Wataka, *you want.*
Ataka, *he or she wants.*
Wataka, *it* [mti] *wants.*
Chataka, *it* [kitu] *wants.*
Twataka, *we want.*
Mwataka, *you want.*
Wataka, *they want.*
Yataka, *they* [miti] *want.*
Vyataka, *they* [vitu] *want.*

The prefixes are the same with the past tense in -ali-, which is used indifferently for the tense in -li-.

Nalitaka *or* Nilitaka, *I wanted.*

Translate into Swahili.

The chief wants a large vessel. The large mango tree fell. This knife wants a large handle. The chief loves old men. The masons want red umbrellas. The trees surround the hut. The bait pleases him. The slaves hated me. The foreigners feared us. The lid covers two cooking pots. They saw the passports. This food pleases. The books arrived. You were born. He boasted. You awoke. The tall trees fell. He shut the door. I love the old man. We hate them. They saw the four black slaves. The four black slaves saw them. The hut pleases me.

THE POSSESSIVE CASE.

There is no true Possessive case in Swahili, it is always represented by the particle -a with

THE POSSESSIVE CASE.

appropriate initial letters, answering very closely to the English word *of*.

The order of the words is the same as when in English the word *of* is used.

    Mji wa mfalme, *the town of the chief.*

The initial letter is determined by the form of the preceding word, that is, of the thing possessed, not of the possessor.

    Kiti cha mzee, *the chair of the old man.*
    Mfuko wa mzee, *the old man's bag.*
    Miti ya mzee, *the old man's trees.*
    Visu vya mzee, *the old man's knives.*

The proper initial letters are, 1. After singular nouns in m-, w-. 2. After plural nouns in wa-, w-. 3. After plural nouns in mi-, y-. 4. After singular nouns in ki- [or ch], ch-. 5. After plural nouns in vi- [or vy-], vy-.

    Mtumwa wa mkalimani, *the interpreter's slave.*
    Watumwa wa kipofu, *the blind man's slaves.*
    Mti wa Mzungu, *the European's tree.*
    Miti ya Wazungu, *the Europeans' trees.*
    Kisu cha kijakazi, *the slave girl's knife.*
    Visu vya walevi, *the drunken men's knives.*

Translate into Swahili.

I took the European's knife. I shall see the chief's town. You will hurt the old man's head. I have found the drunkard's waistcoat. We have passed the European's well. I see the black smoke of a great fire. They are burning the deaf man's books. The chief's slaves took the fisherman's canoe. The slave's knife struck the stranger's arm. They have hidden the canoe's mast. The old man's oath. The stranger's misfortunes. The idle slave's chains. The porters' burdens. The cook's door. The nurse's lips. The children's arrows. The blind man's hut. The mangouste's tail. The mangouste has bitten the child's hand. The European's shoes.

THE POSSESSIVE PRONOUNS.

The Possessive Pronouns consist of an invariable part preceded by the appropriate consonants, which are the same as those used with the particle *a* (of). The invariable parts are

—angu, *my.*   —etu, *our.*
—ako, *thy* or *your.*   —enu, *your.*
—ake, or akwe, *his, hers,*   —ao, *their.*
    or *its.*

The Possessive Pronoun always follows the name of the thing possessed, and changes its initials according to the form of the word it follows.

Mtu wake, *his man.*
Watu wake, *his people.*
Mti wake, *his tree.*
Miti yake, *his trees.*
Kisu chake, *his knife.*
Visu vyake, *his knives.*
Mtu wangu, *my man.*
Watu wako, *your people.*
Miti yetu, *our trees.*
Kisu chenu, *your knife.*
Visu vyao, *their knives.*

Translate into Swahili.

Our chief has killed your slave. The Europeans have cut down their date trees. My cocoanut tree is bearing fruit. His knife [is] sharp. His arrow struck me. Their large vessel has sunk. They liked their food. Our hut has fallen. Your trees please me. The old man wants my waistcoat. My head is paining me. My hand is touching the tree. I see the handle of it. I carried his chain. Your chains [are] heavy. You will take our slaves. I shall leave your arrows. Their actions have pleased us. You [pl.] will hate our chief. Our people hate foreigners. He has hidden my knife. My man is taking your waistcoat. Their spears [are] long. The fisherman's heart [is] light. The smoke of their fire [is] much.

HIM AND HIS.

Where something is done to one person by another which affects one part only or specially, such as striking, binding, &c., the possessive pronoun is used in English, but in Swahili the objective prefix denoting the person is commonly used followed by the name of the part affected.

Alinipiga jicho, *he struck my eye.*
Alinifunga mikono, *he tied my hands.*

Translate into Swahili.

I struck his leg. He hit my head. I tied his legs. They hurt my hands. The mangouste bit his finger. The slaves cut my head. The knife touched my arm. The slave woman rubbed his feet. She scratched my hand. The chief unfastened the slave's hands. He has hurt his own eye. He will tie his own hands.

ALL, HAVING, ITSELF, BY ITSELF.

The words -ote, *all*, -enyi or -inyi, *having*, -enyewe, *-self* or *-selves*, take the same initial letters as those taken by the Possessive Pronouns. *By itself, by myself, by themselves*, &c., is expressed by the word peke followed by the appropriate Possessive pronoun.

Watu wote, *all people*, or *all the people.*
Mti wote, *all the tree*, or *the whole tree.*
Miti yote, *all the trees*, or *all trees.*
Kisu chote, *all the knife*, or *the whole knife.*
Visu vyote, *all the knives*, or *all knives.*

Mtu mwenyi mali, *a man having property.*
Watu wenyi mali, *people with property.*
Mti mwenyi majani, *a tree having leaves.*
Miti yenyi majani, *trees having leaves.*
Kisu chenyi kipini, *a knife with a handle.*
Visu vyenyi vipini, *knives with handles.*

Mimi mwenyewe, *I myself.*
Sisi wenyewe, *we ourselves.*
Mtu mwenyewe, *the man himself.*
Watu wenyewe, *people themselves.*
Mti mwenyewe, *the tree itself.*
Miti yenyewe, *the trees themselves.*
Kisu chenyewe, *the knife itself.*
Visu vyenyewe, *knives themselves.*

ALL, HAVING, ITSELF, BY ITSELF. 33

Mtu peke yake, *the man by himself.*
Watu peke yao, *people by themselves.*
Mimi peke yangu, *I by myself.*
Wewe peke yako, *you by yourself.*
Sisi peke yetu, *we by ourselves.*
Ninyi peke yenu, *you by yourselves.*
Kisu peke yake, *the knife by itself.*
Visu peke yao, *the knives by themselves.*

The word -ote, *all*, has special forms for the first and second persons plural, which are also used in the sense of *together*.

Sisi sote, *we all* or *we together.*
Ninyi nyote, *you all* or *you together.*
Twende sote, *let us go together.*
Wote wawili, *both* or *the two together.*

The word -enyi is used to express the having in any way, and must sometimes be translated by the use of the relative, or of the preposition *with*.

Mtu mwenyi kupenda, *a person having loving,* i.e., *one who loves.*
Miti yenyi kuzaa, *trees having fruitbearing,* i.e., *trees which bear fruit.*
Kitanda chenyi godoro, *a bedstead having a mattress,* i.e., *a bedstead with a mattress.*

Peke with its possessive pronoun may be translated *alone* or *only*.

Translate into Swahili.
All slaves. All things. All trees. All slaves having huts. All things with an end. All

trees by themselves. I saw him by himself. I saw both these people. I am able by myself to lift this waterjar. You (pl.) saw us together. They will all run away. They will throw all the spears. The thieves took all our turbans. We have found them [the turbans] all. I saw three shadows, you saw one only. I saw two baobab trees, you saw them all. I saw the hippopotamus myself. I saw the mountains themselves. The chiefs with turbans told me. A mangouste with a tail. A tree with many thorns. I told the six old men with umbrellas. The chief himself took all the spears with beautiful handles. I stood by myself. We looked together. The spoons ran away by themselves. The wizard saw them [the spoons] all. The wizard cheated both the thieves. They all searched. The whole moon is visible. All the vessels will sink. The books [are] all large.

THE RELATIVE.

The Relative pronoun is expressed by a syllable formed of the letter -o, preceded by the initial consonants proper to its antecedent. The syllable seldom stands alone except in connection with the word -ote, *all*, in the sense of *whichsoever*.

>Mti wo wote, *any tree whatever*.
>Miti yo yote, *any trees whatever*.
>Kitu cho chote, *any thing whatever*.
>Vitu vyo vyote, *any things whatever*.
>Watu wo wote, *any people whoever they may be*.

THE RELATIVE.

When referring to a singular substantive denoting a person, it is most correct to employ *ye* as the relative syllable, though in Zanzibar it is very common to use *o* alone.

Mtu ye yote, *any man.*

The Relative is commonly joined with a verb. It then follows the tense prefix. The tenses with which it is ordinarily used are the present with the prefix -na-, the past with the prefix -li- or -ali- and the future. The prefix of the future when followed by a relative, becomes -taka- instead of -ta-.

When connected with a verb, -o- is always used instead of -wo-.

Mtu anayesimama, *the man who is standing.*
Watu wanaosimama, *the people who are standing.*
Mti unaoanguka, *the tree which is falling.*
Miti inayoanguka, *the trees which are falling.*
Kitu kinachoanguka, *the thing which is falling.*
Vitu vinavyoanguka, *the things which are falling.*

Mtu aliyesimama, *the man who stood.*
Watu waliosimama, *the people who stood.*
Mti ulioanguka, *the tree which fell.*
Miti iliyoanguka, *the trees which fell.*
Kitu kilichoanguka, *the thing which fell.*
Vitu vilivyoanguka, *the things which fell.*

Mtu atakayesimama, *the man who will stand.*
Watu watakaosimama, *the people who will stand.*

THE RELATIVE.

Mti utakaoanguka, *the tree which will fall.*
Miti itakayoanguka, *the trees which will fall.*
Kitu kitakachoanguka, *the thing which will fall.*
Vitu vitakavyoanguka, *the things which will fall.*

The Relative forms for the third person are used also for the first and second, and if an objective prefix is employed it follows the relative.

Niliyemwona, [*I*] *who saw him.*
Uliyemwona, [*you*] *who saw him.*
Tuliomwona, [*we*] *who saw him.*
Mliomwona, [*you*] *who saw him.*

Translate into Swahili.

God who sees me. You who worship God. People who worshipped many gods. A shadow which is passing. Slave women who are carrying water jars. A man who will throw a spear. A spear which will strike me. You who will see the spear. His spear which will kill me. They who know him. They will know the trees which will fall. The trees which will fall will crush your hut. The slave who brought a chair. A chair which was broken. He who broke the chair. His fellow slaves who will beat him. The slave women who will laugh. The simpletons who will run away. The European who will cross the river. The European who will sink. The servants who liked sweet potatoes. The sweet potatoes which are going bad. The vine which is bearing fruit. I saw the date tree which bore fruit. You will see the sore which is

THE RELATIVE.

paining him. The sick people who will wonder. The medicine man who will cure them. The simpletons who will pay the wizard who has cheated them. The chief who loves his wife. The chief who loved his children. The cook who cooked my food. The servant who brought my food. The good food which killed them all.

When the Relative is the object of the verb, the same forms are used and the proper objective prefix is added.

>Mtu niliyemwona, *the man whom I saw.*
>Mti nilioukata, *the tree which I cut down.*
>Mikuke niliyoinunua, *the spears which I bought.*
>Kisu nilichokinunua, *the knife which I bought.*

Translate into Swahili.

The action which you have done. The bedstead which you broke. The bone which he picked up. The book which they took. The boundary which you will pass. The burdens which the porters carried. The chief whom they are killing. The children whom she bore. The door which I am fastening. The Europeans whom you will see. The finger which he bit. The foreigner whom they are beating. The hill which you saw. The hippopotamus which they killed. The hut which he built. The old person whom they pushed. The onions which you (pl.) liked. The piece which you (pl.) will receive. The pole which you will place.

The Relative is much used with interrogatives.

>Aliyenipiga nani? *Who struck me?*
>Nani aliyekuita? *Who called you?*

The particles po, mo, and ko, are treated as

Relatives. Po represents *when, at which,* and *where, of a place near at hand;* mo denotes *within which;* and ko *whither, whence* and *where, of a place far off.*

    Atakapotazama, *when he shall look.*
    Tulimokaa, *within which we sat.*
    Ninakotoka, *whence I come out.*

Translate into Swahili.

When I shall see him. When the foreigner fell. Whither the European is returning. When the date tree will bear. Where we are standing. Whence the black men ran away. The chamber in which he sat down. Where the fishermen overturned our canoe. Where the chief went by. When the old man shall get up. Who saw me? Who is coming out?

THE IMPERATIVE & SUBJUNCTIVE.

The Imperative has only two forms, which are those of the second person, singular and plural. They consist of the simple form of the verb in the singular, to which -ni is added to form the plural.

    Penda, *love.*   Pendani, *love ye.*

In Zanzibar the final -a of the verb is almost always changed into -e.

    Pende, *love.*   Pendeni, *love ye.*

The Subjunctive is formed by changing the final -a into -e and prefixing the proper sign of person.

THE IMPERATIVE AND SUBJUNCTIVE.

Nipende, *that I may love.*
Upende, *that you (thou) may love.*
Apende, *that he (or she) may love.*
   Upende, *that it* (mti) *may love.*
   Kipende, *that it* (kitu) *may love.*

Tupende, *that we may love.*
Mpende, *that you may love.*
Wapende, *that they may love.*
   Ipende, *that they* (miti) *may love.*
   Vipende, *that they* (vitu) *may love.*

The Subjunctive is used for the Imperative and seems to be a somewhat more polite form.

Vuta, *pull.*
Uvute, *please to pull.*
Nitazame, *let me look.*
Atazame, *let him look.*

It is also used with the sense of *Am I* (*Is he, &c.*) *to do* this or that?

Nipite, *Am I to pass?*
Niukate, *Am I to cut it* (mti) *down?*
Achimbe, *Is he to dig?*
Tuvuke, *Shall we cross over?*

In English the purpose with which a thing is done is often expressed by the words *to* or *and*. In Swahili the purpose is always expressed by the Subjunctive.

Call the slaves to help you. Waita watumwa wakusayidie.
Go and look for him. Enenda umtafute.

THE IMPERATIVE AND SUBJUNCTIVE.

Verbs ending in -e, -i, or -u, do not change their final letter in the Subjunctive.

Tuisamehe, pardon me.
Tuisaliki, leave us.
Tujithu, answer us.

Translate into Swahili.

Call the man who beat you, that I may see him. Beat him that he may fear. I have seen the man whom you killed, am I to bury him? I shall accuse him, that I may annoy you. Tell him to answer me. I beg you to believe me. We have agreed to bathe together. Break those cooking pots. Are we to break these knives? Break (pl.) them [the knives] all. Take care of these children. Carry (pl.) these loads. Choose one man to climb up. Cook these sweet potatoes. Collect those sweet potatoes that I may cook them. Tell him to cover the cooking pot. Destroy (pl.) all the huts. We have divided the things which you ordered us to destroy. What are we to do? Let the slave drag the long poles. Let the slave women draw water. Drive the blind man away. Let the deaf man stay. He wants you to help him. He will return to judge the bad men. Pick up the spear which the drunken chief threw to kill me. I tried to kick him. They came near to the tree to climb up it. I followed in order to hinder them. He took off his clothes to bathe. The people ran away that they might escape. The chief sent two slaves to search for me. I turned to uncover the cooking pot. The thief arrived to get the umbrella, my two interpreters went back to hinder him. We three went down to guard the hut.

THE KA- TENSES.

The force of the conjunction *and* is very often given in Swahili by the use of a tense formed with -ka-.

With the Imperative, -ka- is simply prefixed.

>Katupa, *and throw away.*
>Karudi, *and come back.*

With the Subjunctive, -ka- follows the sign of the person.

>Wakarudi, *and let them come back.*
>Akaangalie, *and let him take care.*

To express the past tense preceded by *and*, a tense is formed by the personal prefix followed by -ka-.

>Nikaanguka, *and I fell down.*
>Ukaanguka, *and you [thou] fell down.*
>Akaanguka, *and he [or she fell down.]*
>>Ukaanguka, *and it [mti] fell down.*
>>Kikaanguka, *and it [kitu] fell down.*
>
>Tukaanguka, *and we fell down.*
>Mkaanguka, *and you fell down.*
>Wakaanguka, *and they fell down.*
>>Ikaanguka, *and they [miti] fell down.*
>>Vikaanguka, *and they [vitu] fell down.*

In telling a story, the -ka- tense is used almost universally after the first verb, which is generally in the -li- tense. The chief exceptions are where a verb is joined with a relative particle, or used participially.

Alijiba, akamwambia, *he answered and said to him.*

Alirudi, akafika hata, *he returned and got as far as this (arrived here).*

Translate into Swahili.

And go out [pl.]. And call her. And buy it [pole]. And buy them [poles]. And drive them away [people]. And let him take it [knife.]. Go and help him. Answer me and take care. He went before and arrived. He passed and he returned. He asked me and I told him. She asked you and you told her. Hear [ye] and answer me. You [pl.] looked and saw the trees. I looked for the knife and found it. The slaves found your umbrella which you left and brought it, and I told them, the owner will come back, and they said to me, this man knows him. The foreigners arrived and burnt our town. The European caught my spear and broke it, and I struck him, and he said to the men who followed him, kill that man, and I ran away and escaped. He put on his new shoes and they hurt him. I became tired and my feet swelled. The chief called his men and said to them, this old man is a wizard, hold him, and bind him. And they bound him. And the men who guarded him got drunk and slept, and I unfastened him and he ran away. And the men awoke and said, the wizard has escaped. And they searched for him. And they met with me, and they said to me, You remember the man we bound? And I said to them, which man? And they said to me, That wizard, he has run away, our chief will beat us. And I said to them,

I will show you his town, follow me and you will find him, and I went before and they all followed. And we met with you and you said to us, Go back, the old man has cheated you. The child fell down and cried. He showed me his sore and I cured it. I turned and looked. I took the sweet potato and tasted it. They got drunk and quarrelled. He got up and sang. You [pl.] were sorry and I rejoiced. He waited and I passed.

THE -KI- TENSE.

The case that something is, or is being done, whether actual or supposed, is expressed by a tense formed by the personal prefix and the syllable -ki-. In English this tense is represented by a great number of forms. Frequently by the present participle.

 Nalimwona akioga, *I saw him bathing.*

Frequently by *if.*

 Abdallah akija mwambia, *If Abdallah comes tell him.*

Frequently by *when.*

 Akirudi nitamwona, *when he comes back I shall see him.*

Sometimes by *since* or *because.*

 Akiwa mtu mkuu, siwezi neno, *since he is a great man, I can do nothing.*

THE -KI- TENSE.

Any other form in English in which a state of things is expressed must be translated into Swahili by the use of the -ki- tense.

Translate into Swahili.

If the tree falls. When the tree falls. Suppose the tree should fall. Though the tree fall. While the tree is falling. Though I look. If you look, you will see the black men running away. When the chief arrives, we will tell him. When the knife cuts his finger, the child will cry. When he brings the book, I shall be able to read. If he brings a book which I know. When I hear you speaking, I will answer you. I hear them calling you. On arriving, ask (pl.) him. In going back take care. If you strike me, take care. Supposing he should kill you, I will kill all his children. If his wife kills me he will forgive her. If you love your children, beat them. If you love me forgive them. If the deaf man hears you, tell him. When you bring the blind man we will beat him. Look [pl.] for the thieves, when you find them bring them. When he asks me, you answer him. If I hear him when he calls I shall go back. If I see her looking, I shall hide the water jar. When you see the baobab tree, you have arrived [there]. I see the caravan porters running away, they are leaving their burdens, the strangers as they find them take them. If we delay we shall prosper. When I go back, go back all of you. If we go back, let us go back together. The hut is falling, if we go out we shall escape. Though he run, I shall pass him. If the hut is destroyed, build another. If he makes a canoe, break [pl.] it. If he recollects, we will pay him. If he brings a spear, we will break it. If the cook cooks good food, we will praise him. If he destroys good food, I shall beat him. When she breaks the water-jar, she will fear. While bathing he sank. The European saw him sinking, and ran away. As he lifted his hand, the knife fell, in falling it cut him.

CONDITIONAL TENSE.

Where something would have happened if something else had happened, both branches of the contingency are reprerented by a tense formed by the prefix -ngali- preceded by the proper sign of the person. The condition on which the contingency would have occurred is often marked by the use of the word kama, *if* or *as*.

Mti úngalianguka, *the tree would have fallen.*
Kama níngalikuona níngalikupiga, *If I had seen you, I should have beaten you.*

The accent is always placed on the personal prefix and never on either syllable of the tense prefix -ngali-.

Translate into Swahili.
If I had heard him, I should have feared. If the knife had fallen, it would have cut me. If you had told the chief, he would have killed them. You would have burnt his hut. You [pl.] would have burnt their huts. If their canoes had gone back we should have escaped. The spear would have passed him. The drunkard would have killed his

child. If she had looked, his wife would have seen him. If he had taken care, his wife would have come back. I saw him as he passed, and you said to me, he has made a canoe. And I said to him, this (man) says, you have made a canoe, I want to look at it. And he said to me, if you had asked my slaves, they would have shown you my canoe. And I said to him, show me yourself. And I saw it, and I wondered. If you [pl.] had seen it you would have wondered.

THE NEGATIVE TENSES.

In Swahili the negative of the Verb is made by the use of a special set of prefixes and in one tense by a change in the termination of the Verb.

The negative personal prefixes are—

    I—not—, Si—.
    You [thou] —not—, Hu—.
    He [or she] —not—, Ha—.
        It [mti] *—not—*, Hau—.
        It [kitu] —not—, Haki—.
    We—not—, Hatu—.
    You—not—, Ham—.
    They—not—, Hawa—.
        They [miti] *—not—*, Hai—.
        They [vitu] *—not—*, Havi.

These prefixes are used in forming the Negative Present, Past, Future, and Conditional Tenses and the *Not yet* Tense.

In the Imperative and Subjunctive and with particles of Relation -si- is used in both numbers and with all persons.

NEGATIVE PRESENT.

The negative Present is formed by changing the final -a of the Verb into -i and prefixing the negative prefixes.

Sipendi, *I do not like.*
Hupendi, *You* (thou) *do not like.*
Hapendi, *He* (or *she*) *does not like.*
Haupendi, *It* (mti) *does not like.*
Hakipendi, *It* (kitu) *does not like.*

Hatupendi, *We do not like.*
Hampendi, *You do not like.*
Hawapendi, *They do not like.*
Haipendi, *They* (miti) *do not like.*
Havipendi, *They* (vitu) *do not like.*

Verbs which do not end in -a do not change their final vowel *Is* or *are not*, is expressed by si, for both numbers and all classes of nouns.

Translate into Swahili.

Our chief does not like Europeans. Europeans do not like our medicine men. Idle slaves do not like an overlooker. The river does not pass those baobab trees. I do not see our men. You (pl.) do not like me. I do not hate you (pl.). She is not reading. The canoes are not sinking. You are not taking care. These are writing, those are not.

I said to him, which man is it whom you saw? And he said to me, I do not see him. He is not teaching my children. The old man does not awake. Their children are not crying. Their cocoanut trees are not bearing. My date tree is bearing, yours are not (your date trees are not bearing). He does not like that harpoon. Those masts are falling. His canoe is not sinking. He is not destroying your hut. I do not forget your actions. He does not forgive me. They do not answer us. You do not believe him. He does not consider. They do not order you. I do not praise them. I am not going back. He does not scorn us. You do not suppose. We are not travelling. I do not wonder. They do not worship God. These slaves are not idle.

NEGATIVE PAST.

The Negative past is made by the use of the tense prefix -ku- preceded by the proper negative personal signs, see p. 46.

 Mimi sikuanguka, *I did not fall down.*
 Mti haukuanguka, *the tree did not fall down.*
 Sisi hatukuanguka, *we did not fall down.*
 Vibanda havikuanguka, *the huts did not fall down.*

Translate into Swahili.

I did not accept. We did not agree. I did not answer. The chiefs did not arrive. The Europeans did not buy. The cook did not build. You (pl.) did not buy. Those women did not draw water. The six Europeans did not

NEGATIVE PAST. 49

get drunk. The chief did not go before. The old man did not refuse. The arrow did not hit him. They did not bring the two bedsteads. The Europeans did not cut down the cocoanut trees. The Europeans did not kill six hippopotamus. The interpreter did not show me the islands. The strangers did not build huts. I did not taste the onions. We did not tear the rag. I did not tell the old man. This mason did not use many poles. The cowards did not fear the slave woman. The masons did not want red umbrellas. The slave did not hate her. The books did not arrive. He did not boast. They did not see the four black slaves.

The -ku- tense is used only of an action that is strictly and entirely past. Where the meaning is that something has not been and is not, the present is used.

He has not delayed, hakawii.
He has not prospered, hafanikiwi.
He has not got drunk, halewi.

Where the meaning is that something has not happened as yet, it is expressed by the tense prefix -ja-, preceded by the proper negative personal prefix.

Hajafika, *he has not yet come.*
Sijamwona, *I have not yet seen him.*
Hajaisha (or hajesha), *he has not yet finished.*

The word bado is often added. It seems to imply that the event is one likely to happen, only it has not yet come to pass.

NEGATIVE FUTURE.

Sijamwona bado, *I have not seen him* [*but I think I shall*].
Hajasikia bado, *he has not heard* [*but he will*].
Hajafika bado, *he has not arrived* [*though he is on the way*].

Translate into Swahili.

The foreigner has not yet cut the loaf. The nurse has not yet fed the children. They have not yet brought the two bedsteads. I have not yet seen the book. He has not fastened the chain (as yet). The chiefs have not paid me (as yet). They have not yet passed the children. The date tree has not yet borne. The Europeans have not yet cut down the cocoanut trees. The idle cook has not yet rubbed the lid. The fishermen have not brought the canoe (as yet).

NEGATIVE FUTURE AND CONDITIONAL.

The Negative Future is made by merely prefixing the negative personal signs in place of the ordinary affirmative prefixes.

Nitapenda, *I shall love.*
Sitapenda, *I shall not love.*
Utapenda, *you will love.*
Hutapenda, *you will not love.*
Atapenda, *he will love.*
Hatapenda, *he will not love.*
Tutapenda, *we shall love.*
Hatutapenda, *we shall not love.*

The Negative Conditional is formed in the same manner:

NEGATIVE CONDITIONAL. 51

Níngalipenda, *I should have loved.*
Síngalipenda, *I should not have loved.*
Túngalipenda, *we should have loved.*
Hatúngalipenda, *we should not have loved.*
Ingalianguka, *they (trees) would have fallen.*
Haíngalianguka, *they would not have fallen.*

Translate into Swahili.

He will not go back. We shall not see him. We should not have seen him. If you had not arrived, he would not have seen us. Our chief will not like those Europeans. The Europeans would not have liked our medicine men. Idle slaves would not have liked a sharp overlooker. You (pl.) will not see our men. Europeans would not have slept. Black men would not have fled. The canoes would not have been broken. These cocoanut trees would not have borne. They would not have ordered you. He will not forgive me. We shall not travel. The old man will not go back. Those simpletons will not answer us. I should not have loved him. I should not have told you.

NEGATIVE SUBJUNCTIVE.

The Negative Subjunctive is formed by inserting -si- between the personal sign and the verb; in other respects it resembles the Subjunctive affirmative. It expresses an intention or desire, the object of which is that somebody, or something, may not do or be whatever the verb expresses. It is also used of a purpose which fails, and is the usual

Negative Imperative. The true Negative Imperative is formed when necessary by prefixing Si to the affirmative form, but it is only rarely employed.

> Asipende, *let him not love—that he may not love— without his loving though we desired it.*
> Isianguke, *that they [the trees] may not fall.*

Translate into Swahili.

Let us not see. Let him not go back. That the chief may not tell us. Do not look. Do not look [pl.]. Do not tell him. Beat him that he may not do [it]. Do not speak, that they may not hear [lest they hear]. Tell them not to look for it [book]. Let us not pass it [tree]. Hold the child that she may not fall. Hide the books that they may not read. Tell them not to listen. I will go back that I may not meet with them. Do not pull [pl.]. Tell the porters not to carry these two burdens. Do not take my spear. Do not burn my hut. Do not [pl.] make him a chief. Do not get drunk. Take care the knife does not cut your finger. Take care not to strike that European. Do not praise the slave girls. Do not bring the book, I do not know [how] to read. Do not speak, lest I answer you. If you kill him, do not kill his children.

NEGATIVE WITH RELATIVES.

There is one negative form which is used with the particles of relation for all tenses. It is made by inserting -si- between the personal sign and the sign of relation.

NEGATIVE WITH RELATIVE.

Asiyependa, (*he*) *who does not, did not, or will not love.*
Tusiokupenda, (*we*) *who do not, did not, or will not love you.*
Tusiyekupenda, (*you*) *whom we do not, &c., love.*
Nisiouona, (*the tree*) *which I do not, did not, or shall not see.*
Usiyetuambia, (*thou*) *who didst not, dost not, or wilt not tell us.*

For the signs of relation see p. 36.

The prefixes standing alone express *who is, am,* or *are not, who was, were, will,* or *shall not be.*

Nisiye, (*I*) *who am not, &c.*
Usiye, (*you, thou*) *who are not, &c.*
Wasio, (*they*) *who are not, &c.*

Translate into Swahili.

A shadow which is not passing. Slave women who are not carrying water jars. A man who will not throw a spear. I saw three men, whom you did not see. (You) who will not see the spear, will pass the hut. (They) who do not know him. (I) who did not know him. The trees which did not fall did not crush your hut. The chair which was not broken. Simpletons who will not run away. The European who has not crossed the river. The Europeans who do not cross the river. The servants who not like sweet potatoes. The tree which does not bear fruit. The sick people who do not wonder. The medicine man who will not cure them all. The simpletons who will not pay the wizard who has not cheated them. The chief who does not love his wife. The chief who did not love his children. The cook who did not cook my food. The good food which did not kill us.

NEGATIVE PARTICIPIAL TENSE.

The Negative of the -ki- tense is expressed by the use of the negative -si- with the relative particle -po-, *when.*

Asipopenda, *he not loving,* or *not having loved.*

All the English forms expressed in the affirmative by the -ki- tense may be expressed negatively in Swahili by using -po as a negative relative, and that for past and future time as well as the present.

Asipopenda
{
If he does not love.
If he has not loved.
If he will not love.
When he does, did, or will not love.
Since, because, though, &c. he does, did, or will not love.
}

The syllable -po- being used strictly as a relative particle, all the rules given above for the use of relatives with a negative apply to this case.

Translate into Swahili.

If he does not love you, I shall not love him. If they do not go out, the chief will not come in [enter]. If he will not come near himself, bring him [pl.]. If I do not wait, I shall not get his knife. If the bone is not broken, the arm will get well. Though the European did not kill the cook, he will not please the black people. If you do not beat your child, he will scorn you.

THE PASSIVE VOICE.

The Passive is formed by inserting -w- before the final -a, -e, or -i, of the regular Verb. In all other respects it is the same as the Active.

Napenda, *I love.*
Napendwa, *I am loved.*

Ninapenda, *I am loving.*
Ninapendwa, *I am being loved.*

Nimependa, *I have loved.*
Nimependwa, *I have been loved.*

Nalipenda, *I loved.*
Nalipendwa, *I was loved.*

Nitapenda, *I shall love.*
Nitapendwa, *I shall be loved.*

Nipende, *let me love.*
Nipendwe, *let me be loved.*

Níngalipenda, *I should have loved.*
Níngalipendwa, *I should have been loved.*

Nikipenda, *if I love.*
Nikipendwa, *if I am loved.*

Nikapenda, *and I loved.*
Nikapendwa, *and I was loved.*

THE PASSIVE VOICE.

Sipendi, *I do not love.*
Sipendwi, *I am not loved.*
Sikupenda, *I did not love.*
Sikupendwa, *I was not loved.*
Sitapenda, *I shall not love.*
Sitapendwa, *I shall not be loved.*
Síngalipenda, *I should not have loved.*
Síngalipendwa, *I should not have been loved.*
Nisipende, *that I may not love.*
Nisipendwe, *that I may not be loved.*
Nisiyependa, *I who do not love.*
Nisiyependwa, *I who am not loved.*
Sijapenda, *I have not yet loved.*
Sijapendwa, *I am not yet loved.*

Verbs ending in -e, -i, and -u, and those ending in -oa and -ua, have special passive forms which will be mentioned hereafter. In the last two cases the cause lies, no doubt, in the difficulty of distinguishing between -ua and -uwa, -oa, and -owa. The verbs which do not end in -a are all Arabic words, and therefore more or less irregular.

By after a passive verb is expressed by na.

Nalipigwa na mfalme, *I was beaten by the chief.*

Translate into Swahili.

I was beaten, you were not beaten. He will be beaten by a slave. Let them be beaten. That I may not be beaten. The old man will be bitten. The spear was brought. The two huts are being built. The chief is not yet buried. The slave girls are being called. Let the canoe be taken care of. The Europeans will not be conquered. The food has been cooked. The town has been entered by the four foreigners. The door would have been fastened. I am not feared. The children have not yet been fed. I did not hide the spears, they have been hidden by the owners. If I had told him, I should not be liked by the Europeans. Where has the piece been placed? The wizard is not pleased. You will not be remembered. Your chief will not be remembered by our children. The looking glass has not yet been given back. Let the hut be swept by a slave woman. Let not the children be taught by a European. I was told by his slave. The spear was thrown by the thief.

ADVERBS.

Adverbs in Swahili follow the words they qualify.

Sema sana, *speak loud.*
Mzuri sana, *very beautiful.*

List of Adverbs.

Above, up, on the top, &c., juu.
After, afterwards, behind, &c., baada, baadaye (*time*), nyuma (*place*).
Again, tena.
Altogether, utterly, entirely, quite, kabisa.
Always, sikuzote.
Before, in front, &c., mbele.
Below, at the bottom, chini.

ADVERBS.

Certainly, without a doubt, yakini.
Even, hatta.
Exactly, halisi.
Far, far off, mbali.
Fast, quickly, upesi.
Formerly, long ago, zamani.
Gently, moderately, slowly, polepole.
Gratis, for nothing, idly, burre.
Immediately, marra.
Inside, within, &c., ndani.
Lastly, mwisho.
Merely, only, &c., tu.
More, zayidi.
   More than, zayidi ya.
Near, karibu.
Now, sasa.
   Now directly, sasa hivi.
Often, marra nyingi.
Outside, without, &c., 'nje.
Possibly, yamkini.
Presently, afterwards, then, ultimately, halafu.
Quickly, hastily, hima.
Safely, salama.
Suddenly, unexpectedly, gháfala.
Truly, in truth, sincerely, kweli.
Very, sana. Sana is used to intensify any Verb or Adjective, and may be very variously translated into English.

   Vuta sana, *pull hard.*
   Sema sana, *speak out.*
   Penda sana, *love much.*

Well, properly, thoroughly, vema.
Wonderfully, ajabu.

Translate into Swahili.

I have bought a very handsome spear. He does not see well. I do not much like idle slaves. I saw him coming back fast. I should not have built a very large hut. I looked behind and saw two foreigners. I heard a man near singing loudly (sana), and I thought, this is a European, I will run away (flee) fast. The chief is above, (and) the slaves below. I saw a man looking, and I told you, he sees us now, and you said to me, he is looking outside, we are inside, let us pass gently that he may not hear us, possibly we shall escape; and we passed, and presently another man came out, and I said truly we cannot [kuweza, *to be able*] escape, and you said, he is only a slave, he cannot hinder us, and we passed him. I have often remembered those two people, they would at once have killed us both, if they had known us. The children went before in front, the men followed the children, and last followed the old men.

PREPOSITIONS.

There are in Swahili only four true Prepositions,— na, -a, kwa, and katika.

Na is *with, along with,* and *by* of the agent after a passive Verb. See p. 61, *na* with a pronoun.

-a, *of*, see p. 28.

Kwa denotes instrumentality and object,— *with*, of an instrument; *for, by,* of means; *to,* of a person, or of the place of his residence; *after the manner of, &c.*

Katika is used of place in all its relations, *at, in, to, from, into,* and *out of;* also of an action, *during, in,* or *while.*

Other Prepositions are freely made from Adverbs, &c., by the use of na and -a.

>Pamoja na, *together with.*
>Karibu na, *near [near with].*
>Nyuma ya, *after [at the back of].*
>Mbele ya, *before [in front of].*

A Noun or a Verb may be made into an Adverb by prefixing kwa, and then by the addition of -a the whole becomes a Preposition.

>Sababu, *cause.*
>Kwa sababu, *because [by cause].*
>Kwa sababu ya, *because of.*

The force of the Preposition in English is very generally contained in Swahili in the Verb.

>Kuniletea, *to bring to me.*
>Kumnunulia, *to buy for him.*

Compound Prepositions—

>*Above, on the top of, upon,* juu ya.
>*After (of time),* baada ya.
>*After, behind, at the back of,* nyuma ya.
>*Amidst, in the middle of,* katikati ya.
>*Because,* kwa sababu ya.
>*Before, in front of,* mbele ya.
>*Below, beneath, at the bottom of, under,* chini ya.
>*For, instead of, in place of,* mahali pa.

CONJUNCTIONS. 61

Inside of, within, ndani ya.
Near to, karibu na, karibu ya.
Outside of, nje ya.
Over, juu ya.
Since, tangu.
So far as, up to, till, hatta.

Translate into Swahili.

It [hut] was made of poles. I see a man standing on the canoe. And he received it [kitu] with [his] two hands. I bought the spear for an old rag. He will return from the town. I met with him in the town. Return (pl.) to your chief. He remained upon the tree. And he came down from the tree, and he passed till he met with his two fellow slaves upon another tree. And they arrived at the bottom of the hill. All the slaves followed behind the chief. And he went before with his slaves into the island. I went back to my companions, and we saw the owner in his canoe, and we said to him, come down [shuka] out of your canoe, and he answered, Well, and let us follow our chief quickly, we shall find him in the town. And I said to him, he has not yet arrived in his town, and he said to us, he is now arriving.

CONJUNCTIONS.

The Verbs in Swahili very frequently express what in English is denoted by a Conjunction. The -ka- tenses (p. 41) give the force of *and, but,* or any other word used merely as a connective. *If* and any other words used to introduce a statement or a supposition are expressed by the -ki- tense (p. 43). *In order that*, and all other words denoting purpose or object, are expressed by the use of the Subjunctive. Thus a Conjunction is very seldom used in Swahili immediately before a verb.

List of Conjunctions.

Also, na (*and*), tena (*again*).
Although, kwamba.
And, na. Before a negative, wala *is used instead of* na.

    And I, nami. *And we*, naswi.
    And thou, nawe. *And you*, nanyi.
    And he or *she*, naye.
    And it, [mti] nao, [kitu] nacho.
    And they, [watu] nao, [miti] nayo, [vitu] navyo.

Both — and —, na — na —.
But, lakini (*however*), illa (*but only*), illakini (*except however*), wallakini (*nor however*).
Either — or —, ao — ao —, ama — ama —.
Except, illa.
For, kwani.
However, lakini *beginning the clause*.
If, kwamba.
In order that, illi.
Neither — nor —, wala — wala —.
That (*how that*), kama, kwamba.
Then, baadaye (*afterwards*), kiisha (*this finished*).
Till, hatta.
Too, na. *I too*, &c., see *And I*, &c.
Whether, kwamba, kama.

Translate into Swahili.

A youth and an old man followed me into the town. But the old man stood at the door with a spear, and I said to him, when did you arrive, where have you got that spear, and he did not answer me, and I·asked him again. Immediately I saw also the youth, and I, I asked him where has this old man got that spear. And he said to me, Ask him himself. And I said to him, I have asked him but he does not answer me. And he said to me, perhaps he did not hear you, speak loud. And I spoke loud, and the old man said, I (am) a deaf person, I hear you speaking only, forgive me. And I said to him, and you, forgive me, I did not know. And I asked him again, speaking loud. And he said to me, I bought it. And I said to him, when? And the youth said to me, either he stole (iba) it, or he picked it up in the mountains. And the old man said to him, What do you say? And the youth said, He heard you, and he if he had truly bought it, he would have answered you at once. And I said to him, this (is) an old man, and possibly he has forgotten. And he said to me, he has not forgotten, but we, the people of this town, we know him well, (he is) a thief this, since (he was) a child. And I said to him, what has he stolen? And he said to me, many things, this (man is) a stranger, he was driven away out of his town by his chief, till now he is staying in our town, and we do not like him, but we have not driven him away, because (he is) a wizard, and they the people fear him. And I wondered, hearing him, and I said, I do not believe that this (man is) a wizard, you (are) all cowards and you fear a shadow. And he said to me, I do not fear him, for I think our medicine men are able to conquer him. And I said to the old man, have you heard us? And he said to me, I (am) a deaf man, I only hear you talking; but do not believe him, if he tells you, that I was driven away from my town by our chief. I was not driven away, and I, I shall go back. If.I had been driven away, the people of this town would not have accepted me that I should stay in their town. And I said to him, either you are not a deaf man or certainly he has said truly you (are) a wizard. And the old man said to me, I do not hear. And I turned and went out from the town, and I have not told (any) man except you, but I believe that the old man (was) neither a deaf man, nor a wizard, but a cunning man, who had stolen the spear, and wished to cheat me, but I too, I know (how) to cheat people.

OTHER CLASSES OF NOUNS.

The other Classes of Nouns of most importance are those which do not change to form the plural and those which form their plural by prefixing ma-. The remaining three are of less importance, they are those which begin in the singular with u- or w-, the Infinitives of Verbs used as Substantives, and the one word Mahali, *place*. As the rules in regard to these two last are very simple, they may each be despatched in a single article.

PLACE.

The formative syllable appropriate to the

word mahali is -pa-, and as it belongs exclusively to this word its mere presence is enough to show that *place* is the substantive referred to, so that the word mahali may often be omitted.

1. Adjectives are made to agree with mahali by prefixing pa-.

Mahali papana, *a broad place.*

When followed by -e- or -i- the -a- coalesces with it into the sound of -e-.

Mahali peusi, *a black place.*

For lists of Adjectives see pp. 4 and 25.

2. *This place* and *yonder place* are formed on the syllable -pa-: hapa, *this place* or *here*, pale, *that place* or *there.*

3. The signs of person and object in connection with place are both -pa-.

Panipendeza, *it pleases me.*
Napaona, *I see it.*

4. The initial syllable of the Interrogatives and Personal Pronouns is pa-, varying as mentioned above (1).

Mahali papi? *Which place?*
Mahali pangapi? *How many places?*
Mahali pangu, *my place.*
Mahali petu, *our place* or *places.*

5. The sign of the possessive case is pa.

Mahali pa Abdallah, *Abdallah's place.*

F

6. *All* is pote-; *having*, penyi; *itself*, penyewe.

Mahali pote penyi miti, *all places with trees*.

7. The Relative particle answering to mahali is -po-. It often has the sense of *where*.

Nilipopaona, *which I saw*.

Translate into Swahili.

I saw the place where the fisherman stood when (-ki- tense) their new canoe sank. I passed the place itself. I saw a place where there were (having) many huts. Suleman arrived in your place, and I asked him, where did you leave Abdallah, tell me the place, and he told me the place in the town, where his elders (old persons) lived before. And I said to him, I do not know it. And he told me, where you saw him, in crossing the river. And I remembered the place, (it was a) beautiful (one) near the river. And I said to him, now I remember it, we saw it together, (it is a) beautiful place. And he said to me, (it is) beautiful.

INFINITIVES OF VERBS.

Infinitives may always be used in Swahili as verbal substantives expressing the act of doing or becoming, or the state of being, what the verb describes.

Kufa, *dying or becoming dead*.
Kupigana, *fighting*.
Kustirika, *being covered*.

Adjectives and Pronouns are brought into agreement by the use of the syllable -ku-.

Kufa kuzuri, *a noble death.*
Kupigana si kwema, *fighting is not good.*
Kuogopa huku, *this fearing.*
Kuja kwake kumenipendeza, *his coming has pleased me.*
Hakukunipendeza kukimbia kwako, *your running away did not please me.*
Nimekujua kulewa kwako, *I know of your getting drunk.*

Translate into Swahili.

Accepting. Accusing. Agreeing. Altering. I do not like beating you. Answering often. Bearing fruit much. Seeing and believing. Boasting is not good. Boiling quickly. Bringing is not taking. Her cooking (is) beautiful. Crying will harm you. By (means of) cultivating. While dancing. By digging deep (sana). By beautiful dreaming and bad doing. The idle slave annoys me much by his delaying. They brought the trees by dragging. He escaped because of fearing. I saw them while (in) fighting. Forgiving and forgetting.

THE MA- CLASS.

Nouns which make their plural by prefixing ma- have no prefix in the singular unless the roots are monosyllabic, when they prefix ji-, or begin with a vowel, when they ordinarily prefix j-. There are many nouns beginning with ma- which are seldom or never used in the singular.

List of Substantives of the ma- class.

Machukio, *abhorrence, disgust.*
Shauri, mashauri, *advice.*
Jambo, mambo, *affair, thing, circumstance.*
Mapenzi, *affection, love.*
Maagano, *agreement.*
Mapatano, *agreement.*
Koonde, makoonde, *a slave's allotment.*
Lozi, malozi, *an almond.*
Talasimu, matalasimu, *an amulet.*
Mazumgumzo, *amusement, conversation.*
Jibu, majibu, *an answer.*
Tao, matao, *an arch.*
Kwapa, makwapa, *the armpit.*
Jifu, majifu, *ashes.*
Makusanyiko, *assembly, place of assembly.*
Shoka, mashoka, *an axe.*
Kanda, makanda, *a long narrow matting bag.*
Peto, mapeto, *a small square matting bag.*
Fungu, mafungu, *a bank, a shoal.*
Ganda, maganda, *bark, rind.*
Pipa, mapipa, *a barrel.*
Bakuli, mabakuli, *a basin.*
Pakacha, mapakacha, *a basket plaited out of fresh cocoanut leaves.*
Ungo, maungo, *a flat basket for sifting.*
Tuta, matuta, *a raised bed for planting sweet potatoes.*
Tumbo, matumbo, *belly, entrails, womb.*
Lengelenge, malengelenge, *a blister.*
Jipu, majipu, *a boil.*
Chupa, machupa, *a bottle* [*in the Mombas dialect,* tupa, matupa].
Kasha, makasha, *a large box, a chest.*
Tawi, matawi, *a branch, a bunch of fruit.*
Gari, magari, *a carriage, a cart.*

THE MA- CLASS.

Korosho, makorosho, *a cashew nut.*
Bibo, mabibo, *a cashew apple.*
Zizi, mazizi, *a cattle pen.*
Kapi, makapi, *chaff.*
Kanisa, makanisa, *a Church.*
Wingu, mawingu, *a cloud.*
Kuti, makuti, *a leaf of the cocoanut tree.*
Dafu, madafu, *a cocoanut in the proper stage for drinking.*
Makumbi, *cocoanut fibre.*
Agizo, maagizo, *commission, direction.*
Matumaini, *confidence.*
Shaka, mashaka, *doubt.*
Tone, matone, *a drop.*
Vumbi, mavumbi, *dust.*
Sikio, masikio, *an ear.*
Yayi, mayayi, *an egg.*
Jicho, macho, *an eye.*
Kosa, makosa, *a fault.*
Konde, makonde, *a fist.*
Ua, maua, *a flower.*
Inzi, mainzi, *a fly.*
Tunda, matunda, *fruit.*
Tawa, matawa, *a frying pan.*
Tango, matango, *a gourd eaten like cucumber.*
Kaburi, makaburi, *a grave, a tomb.*
Jembe, majembe, *a hoe.*
Tundu, matundu, *a hole.*
Gote, magote, *the knee.*
Fundo, mafundo, *a knot.*
Maneno, *language.*
Jani, majani, *a leaf.*
Soko, masoko, *market, bazaar.*
Jamvi, majamvi, *coarse matting.*
Maziwa, *milk.*
Jina, majina, *name.*

Shingo, mashingo, *the neck.*
Kasia, makasia, *an oar.*
Mafuta, *oil.*
Chungwa, machungwa, *an orange.*
Kafi, makafi, *a paddle.*
Papayi, mapapayi, *a papaw.*
Kokoto, makokoto, *a small piece of stone, a pebble.*
Manukato, *perfumes.*
Nanasi, mananasi, *a pine apple.*
Shimo, mashimo, *a pit.*
Shamba, mashamba, *a plantation, a piece of ground in the country.*
Sufuria, masufuria, *a large metal pot.*
Boga, maboga, *a pumpkin.*
Majuto, *regret, repentance.*
Tanga, matanga, *a sail.*
Jiwe, mawe, *a stone.*
Jifya, mafya, *stones to set a pot on over a fire.*
Jua, *the sun.*
Jino, meno, *a tooth.*
Mumunye, mamumunye, *vegetable marrow.*
Dau, madau, *a small vessel sharp at both ends.*
Mashairi, *verses.*
Maji, *water.*
Tikiti, matikiti, *a wild water melon.*
Neno, maneno, *a word.*

ADJECTIVES [MA- CLASS].

Adjectives beginning with a consonant (p. 4) are made to agree with nouns of the ma- Class by omitting all prefix in the singular and prefixing ma- in the plural.

Sufuria tupu, *an empty pot.*
Mawe makubwa, *large stones.*
Yayi bovu, *a rotten egg.*
Maji matamu, *sweet water.*

ADJECTIVES [MA- CLASS].

Adjectives beginning with a vowel [p. 26] prefix j- to form the singular and ma- to form the plural. The -a- of the prefix ma- coalesces with i or e to form a long e.

>Shauri jerevu, *cunning advice.*
>Maganda meusi, *black bark.*
>Dafu jingine, *another cocoanut.*
>Madafu mengi, *many cocoanuts.*
>Mavazi meupe, *white dresses.*

Translate into Swahili.

A bad affair. Great affection. Ripe almonds. A sharp answer. A wide arch. Dry ashes. A heavy axe. Thick barks. A small barrel. A sound basin. Long raised beds for sweet potatoes. Large blisters. New boils. Empty bottles. A heavy chest. A sweet cocoanut for drinking. A large drop. Long ears. Rotten eggs. New faults. Savage flies. Sweet fruits. An empty grave. A small hole. Fine language. A long leaf. Short leaves. A broad mat. Raw milk. A beautiful name. A long neck. Heavy oars. Sweet oranges. Fine perfumes. A large plantation. Beautiful verses.

A soft knee. A narrow hole. Another grave. Many graves. Much [many] water. A red fruit. Long red fruit. Slender flies. Different faults. Black eyes. Light eyes. A red eye. A white egg. Light dust [pl.]. Many doubts. A small narrow dau. Good confidence. Good red bottles. A light basin. A good axe. Good light axes. Cunning answers. Good almonds. Easy affairs.

DEMONSTRATIVES [MA- CLASS].

The pronominal syllables answering to Substantives of the ma- class are *li* in the singular and *ya* in the plural.

The Demonstratives are made as explained on page 8, and are *hili* and *lile*, *haya* and *yale*.

Kasha hili, *this chest*.
Kasha lile, *that chest*.
Makasha haya, *these chests*.
Makasha yale, *those chests*.

Translate into Swahili.

This large chest. Those large metal cooking pots. These gourds [matango]. Those long ears. This small fault. That hole. These knees. These light drops. Those bitter doubts. This large eye. These large teeth. This large raw egg. That raw egg. Those bottles. These commissions. These boils. Those four large barrels. These dry ashes. These five arches. That answer. These white almonds. This good advice. These new circumstances. That sweet water. These sharp axes. That sharp axe. That barrel. This barrel.

WHICH? [MA- CLASS].

The Interrogative *which?* is formed by prefixing the pronominal syllables to the invariable *-pi*.

Jambo lipi? *Which matter?*
Mambo yapi? *Which matters?*

Translate into Swahili.

Which bottles? Which chest? Which ear? Which eggs? Which eye? Which fruits? Which hole? Which pit? Which knee? Which barrels? Which axe? Which oars? Which shoal? Which water? Which oil? Which arch? Which tooth?

PERSONAL PRONOUNS [MA-CLASS].

The Pronominal syllables may be used alone to represent the present tense of the verb to be.

Kasha li zito, *the chest is heavy.*
Makasha ya mazito, *the chests are heavy.*

The same syllables form the personal prefix to the Verb. See pp. 11, 12, 15.

Dafu limeanguka, *the cocoanut has fallen.*
Madafu yameanguka, *the cocoanuts have fallen.*

They are also used as objective prefixes to mark the object of the Verb. See p. 21.

Wapagazi hawakulichukua kasha, *the porters did not carry the chest.*
Wapagazi hawakuyachukua makasha, *the porters did not carry the chests.*

Before a vowel the vowels of the prefix disappear. See pp. 24 and 27.

Jicho lataka kuoshwa, *the eye wants to be washed.*
Macho yataka kuoshwa, *the eyes want to be washed.*

Translate into Swahili.

I have accepted the advice. These circumstances do not agree. You will not alter the agreement. The ashes annoy me. The matting bags (kanda) have arrived. The water is boiling. He has broken the basin. Bring (pl.) six barrels. Who has built the tomb? Let us break the axe. Buy ten eggs. Do not break the eggs. Let them take care of the frying pan. The women will carry the water in water jars. I like to chew this sweet bark. They have not cleaned the matting. We collected the oranges. Our cook will cook the pineapples. Cover the metal pot. They have crushed the almonds. Are we to cut the blister? The milk is decreasing. The slaves tried to defend the cattle pen. Are we to divide the papaws, or the cashew nuts? They emptied out the oil. The chief did not enter the pit. You will find the two pumpkins at the door. They forgot to bring the oars, they brought only two paddles. If they had hoisted the sail, they would have escaped. If they had not hoisted the large sail, they would not have sunk. We are looking for the wild water melons, have you seen them?

POSSESSIVE PRONOUNS AND CASE [MA- CLASS].

The preposition *of* is made to agree with ma- nouns by the use of the initials l- and y-. See p. 29.

The same initials mark the agreement of the Possessive Pronouns. See p. 30.

POSSESSIVE PRONOUNS & CASE [MA-CL.]. 75

 Kasha la Ali, *Ali's chest.*
  Kasha langu, *my chest.*
 Makasha ya Ali, *Ali's chests.*
  Makasha yangu, *my chests.*
 Jina lake, *his name.*
  Majina yake, *his names.*
 Jina lao, *their name.*
  Majina yenu, *your names.*

Similarly, *all* is *lote* in the singular, and *yote* in the plural. *Having, &c.*, is *lenyi* and *yenyi*, *itself* is *lenyewe*, and *themselves, yenyewe.* See p. 32.

 All the boxes, makasha yote.
  The whole box, kasha lote.
 The basin with eggs, bakuli lenyi mayayi.
  The basins with eggs, mabakuli yenyi mayayi.
 The tooth itself, jino lenyewe.
  The teeth themselves, meno yenyewe.

Translate into Swahili.

I took the European's axe. I shall see the chief's plantation. You will hurt the old man's eye. I have found the drunkard's paddle. We have passed the European's grave. I see the white ashes of a great fire. They are burning the deaf man's pineapples. The chief's slaves took the fisherman's paddles. The slave's knee struck the stranger's eye. They have hidden the canoe's sail. The old man's neck. The stranger's regret. The idle slave's belly. The porters' agreement. The cook's metal pot. The nurse's affection. The children's teeth. The blind man's advice [pl.].

The mangouste's ear. The mangouste has bitten the child's armpit. The European's answer.

Our chief has destroyed your plantation. The Europeans have cut their cocoanut leaves. My fruit [is] ripe. His axe [is] sharp. His arrow struck my neck. They liked their oranges. Our arch has fallen. Your slave girls took my frying pan. Your vegetable marrows please me. The old man wants my amulet. My tooth is paining me. My axe is touching the tree. I see its hole. I carried his oranges. Your boil [is] large. You will take our perfumes. I shall leave your carriage. Their conversation has pleased me. You [pl.] will hate our flies. Our people like papaws. He has hidden my milk. Your verses [are] many. Our milk, your [pl.] water, and their oil. My abhorrence, your affection, and their regret. Our agreement is not yet ended. My blister is not your boil.

All affairs. All amusement. The answer itself. The barrels themselves. The barrels with water. The barrel with oil. The raised bed with sweet potatoes. All boils hurt me. Bring all the basins. The ear itself. Break all the leaves and bring all the fruit. Language having faults.

THE RELATIVE [MA- CLASS].

The Relative particles answering to the ma- class are *lo* in the singular and *yo* in the plural. See pp. 34-38, and 53.

Pipa lo lote, *any barrel whatever.*
Mapipa yo yote, *any barrels whatever.*

Jino linalouma, *the tooth which is aching.*
Jino lililouma, *the tooth which ached.*
Jino litakalouma, *the tooth which will ache.*
　Meno yanayouma, *the teeth which are aching.*
　Meno yaliyouma, *the teeth which ached.*
　Meno yatakayouma, *the teeth which will ache.*
Sufuria nililolinunua, *the pot I bought.*
Masufuria niliyoyanunua, *the pots I bought.*

Translate into Swahili.

The disgust which I feel (see). The advice which I received. The circumstances which annoyed me. The agreement which we made, you and I. The almonds which were picked up. The answer which he will give (put out). The arch which is falling. The ashes which he is scattering. The axe which will cut (down) that tree. The barrels which the chief's people carried. The basin which I broke. The blister which pained me. The boil which was visible. The cart which they are drawing. The church which we are building in the town. The confidence which the slaves will feel (see). The flies which are annoying me. The oil which you are pouring. The pit which you dug. The perfumes which you bought. The pineapples which are being cooked. The wild water melons which the children are looking for. The sail which they hoisted.

NEGATIVE TENSES [MA- CLASS].

The negative prefixes answering to ma- nouns are *hali-* in the singular and *haya-* in the plural. In the Negative Subjunctive, the prefixes become *lisi-* and *yasi-*.

See pp. 46-55.

Tone halianguki, *the drop does not fall.*
    Matone hayaanguki, *drops do not fall.*
Tanga halikushushwa, *the sail was not lowered.*
    Matanga hayakushushwa, *the sails were not lowered.*
Jino halitauma, *the tooth will not ache.*
    Meno hayatauma, *the teeth will not ache.*
Yayi lisioze, *that the egg may not go bad.*
    Mayayi yasioze, *that the eggs may not go bad.*
Boga lisilopikwa, *the pumpkin which was not cooked.*
    Maboga yasiyopikwa, *the pumpkins which were not cooked.*

Translate into Swahili.

Our chief does not like these almonds. These circumstances do not annoy me. This axe does not cut. These amusements do not please me. His answer does not suffice. The barrel is not sinking. The eye does not hear. The ear does not see. Pumpkins do not fly. Vegetable marrows do not cry.

The basin did not arrive. The axe did not hurt me. The amulet did not harm him. Their amulets did not guard them. The bitter bark did not cure you.

The affair is not yet finished. The bitter bark has not as yet cured you. The drop has not yet fallen. The eggs are not yet cooked. The water has not boiled as yet. The leaf has not yet got dry.

A sharp answer will not drive him away. The pine apples will not go bad. These verses will not please him much. Your verses will not please the chief. Hard language will not kill us. Regret will not pay me. The sails will not touch the mast.

Let not the eggs go bad. That the oranges may not fall. That the pumpkins may not be cooked. That the fruit (pl.) may not be crushed. That the ashes be not taken care of. [Do] not [let] the eggs fall.

THE N CLASS.

Substantives which have n- or ny- for a prefix do not change to form the plural.

>Nyumba, *a house.*
>Nyumba, *houses.*
>Ndoo, *a bucket.*
>Ndoo, *buckets.*

The letter *n* cannot, however, stand before any letters except *d, g, j, y,* and *z*. Before *b* and *v* it becomes *m*.

>Mbaya *stands for* nbaya (*bad*).
>Mvua *stands for* nvua (*rain*).

When prefixed to *w* the two letters become *mb*.

>Mbili *stands for* nwili (*two*).

When prefixed to *l* or *r* they become *d*.

>Ndimi *stands for* nlimi (*tongues*).
>Ndefu *stands for* nrefu (*long*).

THE N CLASS.

When *n* ought to be prefixed to *k, p,* or *t,* it is not written, but the letters get a sort of explosive sound, which may be heard in such words as

>K'uku *for* nkuku, *a fowl.*
>P'epo, *for* npepo, *winds.*
>T'aka *for* ntaka, *dirt.*

Before vowels the prefix takes the form *ny-*.

>Nyekundu *for* nekundu, *red.*

These rules make it difficult to know what Substantives ought to be reckoned as belonging to the *n-* class. The difficulty is increased by the custom of putting foreign words into this class whatever their form.

It is a good general rule for a beginner to reckon as belonging to this class all nouns as to which he is uncertain how to class them. He will very often be right, and the only mistake he can make in the noun is to omit a prefix, which is better than putting a wrong one, while the forms of the pronoun are sure to convey his meaning, which other forms might not.

List of *N* Substantives.

Hesabu, *accounts.*
Daftari, *account book.*
Hewa, *air.*
Sadaka, *alms, offering.*
Amerikano, *American sheeting.*
Nanga, *an anchor.*
Hasira, *anger.*

THE N CLASS.

Pembe, *angle, corner.*
Nyama, *animal, meat, flesh.*
Chungu, *ants.*
Siafu, *brown ants often seen crossing the path in great numbers.*
Mchwa, *white ants.*
Nyani, *ape.*
Nguvu, *authority, strength, power.*
Tufe, *a ball.*
Farumi, *ballast.*
Ndizi, *bananas.*
Ng'ambo, *the opposite bank.*
Boriti, *roof beam, pole.*
Ndevu, *beard.*
Kengele, *bell.*
Jeneza, *bier.*
Damu, *blood.*
Ndoo, *bucket, pail.*
Ngao, *buckler, shield.*
Shughuli, *business, engagement.*
Siagi, *butter, cream.*
Ulayiti, *English unbleached calico.*
Kaniki, *blue calico.*
Shiti, *printed calico.*
Galawa, *a canoe.*
Kofia, *a cap.*
Shehena, *cargo.*
Zulia, *a carpet.*
Khalfati, *caulking.*
Nasibu, *chance, luck, good fortune.*
Sifa, *character, praise.*
Nathari, *choice.*
Saa, *clock, watch, hour.*
Nguo, *cotton cloth, a loin cloth, clothes.*
Joho, *woollen cloth, an Arab coat.*

G

THE N CLASS.

Garofuu, *cloves.*
Rungu, *club.*
Nazi, *a cocoanut (when ripe).*
Kahawa, *coffee.*
Rangi, *colour, dye, paint.*
Hali, *condition, state.*
Sandarusi, *copal or gum animi.*
Shaba, *copper, brass.*
Pembe, *corner, horn, angle.*
Pamba, *cotton.*
Thiraa, *a cubit, about half a yard.*
Dasturi, *custom.*
Tende, *dates.*
Siku, *day (in reckoning).*
Deni, *debt.*
Sitaha, *deck.*
Tofauti, *difference.*
Shidda, *difficulty, distress, trouble.*
Aibu, *disgrace, reproach.*
Talaka, *divorce.*
Ndoto, *dream.*
Ngoma, *drum, drumming, music, dance.*
Inchi [*Mombas,* nti], *earth, land, country.*
Raha, *east, rest, comfort.*
Bidii, *effort, strong attempt.*
Njaa [*Mombas,* ndaa], *famine, hunger.*
Hofu, *fear, dread.*
Tupa, *a file.*
Bandera, *flag, red stuff.*
Nyama, *flesh, meat, animal.*
Nguvu, *force, strength, authority.*
Fayida, *gain, profit, advantage.*
Bustani, *a garden.*
Samli, *ghee, clarified butter.*
Zawadi, *a gift, especially a token of remembrance.*

THE N CLASS. 83

ıabu, *gold.*
ʒu, *ground nuts.*
duki, *a gun.*
ıti, *gunpowder.*
u, *half.*
ı, *handkerchief.*
ı, *health, good health.*
ma, *the hold of a ship.*
li, *honey, syrup.*
hima, *honour, respect.*
mba, *a house.*
ımu, *image, likeness, idol.*
ri, *a journey, voyage.*
ıha, *joy.*
i, *justice, right.*
ına, *kind, sort, pattern.*
zi, *a ladder.*
, *a lamp.*
ria, *law, rule.*
ısi, *lead.*
ıu, *learning, doctrine.*
ıa, *letter, note, document.*
u, *light.*
kaa, *lime.*
ara, *loss, damage.*
ıe, *a mango.*
na, *a mark.*
na, *meaning.*
·a, *medicine.*
ıa, *money, silver.*
u, *mosquito.*
lano, *a needle.*
ari [pl.], *news.*
ti, *noise, voice, sound.*
, *the nose.*

THE N CLASS.

Hesabu, *number.*
Asili, *origin, nature, substance.*
Karatasi, *paper.*
Amani, *peace.*
Lulu, *a pearl.*
Kalamu, *a pen.*
Nguzo, *pillar, column, post.*
Sahani, *a plate.*
Ncha, *point, thin end.*
Sumu, *poison.*
Thamani, *price, value.*
Fayida, *profit.*
Ahadi, *promise.*
Robo, *a quarter.*
Mvua, *rain.*
Dini, *religion, worship.*
Haja, *request, desire.*
Mali, *riches, property, possessions.*
Dari, *roof, upper floor.*
Nafasi, *room, space, time, opportunity.*
Kamba, *rope.*
Kutu, *rust.*
Parafujo, *a screw.*
Bahari, *the sea.*
Siri, *a secret, secresy, mystery.*
Akili, *sense, intellect, wits.*
Haya, *shame, modesty.*
Merikebu, *a ship.*
Dalili, *sign, mark, evidence.*
Ishara, *sign, signal.*
Ngozi, *skin, hide, leather.*
Ndui, *small pox.*
Sabuni, *soap.*
Roho, *soul, life.*
Nyota, *a star.*

Hali, *state, health, circumstances.*
Fimbo, *a stick.*
Meza, *a table.*
Lami, *tar.*
Durubini, *a telescope.*
Hema, *a tent.*
Kiu, *thirst.*
Handaki, *a trench, a ditch.*
Hila, *a trick, stratagem, device.*
Mboga [pl.], *vegetables.*
Siki, *vinegar.*
Njia [*Mombas* ndia], *way, road, means.*
Kabari, *a wedge.*
Ngano, *wheat.*
Ajabu, *wonder, a wonder.*
Kazi, *work, employment, function.*
Jeraha, *a wound.*
Dawati, *writing desk.*
Foramali, *a ship's yard.*

ADJECTIVES [N CLASS].

Adjectives agreeing with Substantives of the n class are formed according to the same rules, and have the plural the same as the singular.

Adjectives beginning with a vowel [p. 25] prefix ny-.

Nyumba nyekundu, *a red house,* or *red houses.*
Alama nyekundu, *a red mark,* or *red marks.*

Adjectives beginning with a consonant [p. 4], are formed as follows.

-zuri, *beautiful, fine* — nzuri.
-geni, *foreign, strange* — ngeni.
-gumu, *hard* — ngumu.

THE N CLASS.

-zito, *heavy* — nzito.
-dogo, *little* — ndogo.
-zima, *sound, whole, perfect* — nzima.
-refu, *long* — ndefu.
-baya, *bad* — mbaya.
-bichi, *raw, fresh* — mbichi.
-bivu, *ripe* — mbivu.
-bovu, *rotten* — mbovu.
-tupu, *bare, empty* — tupu.
-chungu, *bitter* — chungu.
-pana, *broad* — pana.
-kuu, *chief, great* — kuu.
-kavu, *dry* — kavu.
-chache, *few* — chache.
-kali, *fierce, sharp* — kali.
-kubwa, *great* — kubwa.
-fupi, *short* — fupi.
-tamu, *sweet* — tamu.
-nene, *thick* — nene.
-kukuu, *worn out* — kukuu.

Three common adjectives are more or less irregular.
    -ema, *good*, makes njema *or* ngema.
    -pya, *new*, makes 'mpya.
    -wazi, *open*, makes wazi.

The variable numbers are formed as follows [see p. 6].

One, moja.	*Two*, mbili.
Three, tatu.	*Four*, 'nne.
Five, tanu.	*Eight*, nane.

Translate into Swahili.
Many great losses. Two ripe mangoes. A black

THE N CLASS. 87

mark. White silver. One mosquito. Sharp needles. Good news. A long nose. Eight letters. Beautiful pearls. A good pen. A thick pillar. Sharp points. Large prices. Three quarters. A new request. Good roofs. Much space. Many opportunities. Red rust. Long screws. Little (few) sense. A plain (open) sign. Large hides. Soft soap. Small stars. A bad state. A long stick. Broad tables. White tents. A cunning trick. A short way. Ripe wheat. A fine writing desk. Heavy anchors. Three corners. Raw flesh. Great (many) authority. Sweet bananas. A long beard. Black blood. Small buckets. A large carpet. A good character. Heavy clubs. White paint. Six cubits. Ten days. A narrow deck. Many dreams. New flags. Beautiful gardens.

PRONOUNS [N CLASS].

The pronominal syllables answering to the N class are *i* in the singular and *zi* in the plural.

1. These syllables standing alone represent the present tense of the verb *to be*.

>Nyumba i kubwa, *the house is large*.
>Nyumba zi kubwa, *the houses are large*.

2. They form the personal and objective prefixes to the verb.

>Nyumba imeanguka, *the house has fallen down*.
>Nyumba zimeanguka, *the houses have fallen down*.
>Nimeinunua nyumba, *I have bought the house*.

Nimezinunua nyumba, *I have bought the houses.*

3. Before a vowel they become *y-* and *z*.

Fayida yapita kiburi, *profit surpasses pride.*
Akili zapita mali, *understanding* (pl.) *surpasses property.*

Translate into Swahili.

Accounts annoy me. Profit pleases me. They received the offerings. The anchor is heavy. He struck the corner. The animals have run away. He is looking for the animals. The ants [siafu] have bitten us. The white ants have destroyed the account books. The roof beams are long. I have heard the bell. Four men are carrying the bier. The blood will remind me. I saw the two empty buckets. I put on the cap, and it hurt me. And the clock struck. The clothes want to be fastened. I bought the cloves. And the dream was finished. Hunger is hurting me. They will hoist the flag. The flag has been hoisted. I did not get the profit. I have got the loss. We hear the noise.

DEMONSTRATIVES [N CLASS].

The demonstratives are formed from the pronominal syllables as explained at p. 9. They are *hii* and *ile, hizi* and *zile.*

Nyumba hii, *this house.*
Nyumba ile, *that house yonder.*
Nyumba hizi, *these houses.*
Nyumba zile, *those houses.*

POSSESSIVES [N CLASS].

The interrogative *which?* is in the singular *ipi*, and in the plural *zipi*.

Translate into Swahili.

The house [is large]. This garden [is] little. This great wonder. These two heavy wedges. This sharp vinegar. Yonder signal. Which signals? Those dry hides. Those beautiful pearls. These sweet mangoes. This new money. Which needles? This request. These lamps. Which lamps? These. This gunpowder. Those tents. This country. Which bucket? This carpet. Those caps. Those houses. This clock. These clothes.

POSSESSIVES [N CLASS].

The preposition *of* is made to agree with nouns of the N class by using y in the singular and z in the plural as initial letters.

Nyumba ya Abdallah, *Abdallah's house.*
Nyumba za Abdallah, *Abdallah's houses.*

The same letters are used as the initials for the possessive pronouns.

Nyumba yake, *his house.*
Nyumba zake, *his houses.*

All, having, itself, and *themselves,* are formed in a similar manner, becoming *yote, yenyi,* and *yenyewe,* in the singular—*zote, zenyi,* and *zenyewe* in the plural.

All the house, Nyumba yote.
All the houses, Nyumba zote.

The house with a door, Nyumba yenyi mlango.
Houses with doors, Nyumba zenyi milango.

Translate into Swahili.

I have seen his accounts. Show me your account book. Abdallah's profits pass mine. I have bought all his bananas. The roof beams of my house. He cut the old man's beard. The children are ringing (striking) our two bells. He let down our bucket into your well. Abdallah's spear struck Ali's shield. Our business (pl.) (is) much. Mabruki has put on my red cap. My watch (is) good, his (is) bad. His cloth is torn. Those dates (are) mine. Our good dreams. Your (pl.) files. Your (pl.) lamps are burning. I did not accept his gold. I have not yet seen your ground nuts. We do not worship their images. They saw your (pl.) tents. I do not hear their voices. They will not get their request. He will not tell me his secrets. Do your work. The medicine man is not able (does not know) to cure their wounds.

I hate all presents. All presents please our chief. A garden with (having) trees. Tents with flags. All the bananas are (have) gone bad. All the butter has melted.

THE RELATIVE [N CLASS].

The Relative particles answering to the *n* class are *-yo-* in the singular and *-zo-* in the plural.

The house which fell, nyumba iliyoanguka.
The houses which fell, nyumba zilizoanguka.

The house which I bought, nyumba niliyoinunua.
The house I did not buy, nyumba nisiyoinunua.
See pp. 33, 37, and 53.

Translate into Swahili.

The wound which I cured. The wounds which I did not cure. The star which followed. You saw the work which they did. The wheat which will be ground. The wedge which our man put under the door was loosened. The vinegar which did not go bad was spilt. The trench which he dug in his plantation reached as far as the house which you bought. I saw the signs which I was told to notice [angalia]. His modesty has left him. Look for the screws we saw yesterday [jana]. The rust which is visible to-day (leo) was visible yesterday. All requests which the chief shall withhold to-day, I will hear afterwards. The room which I wanted would have sufficed you. The rain which passed over our roof got [entered] into the new house which they are building. The promise which I gave [put out]. The chief knew the trick which deceived the foreigners. The money which the fisherman received [was] much [many]. I shall give [put out] a quarter of the price which the mason wants. The pillars which were crushed [were] all large. The pearl which the fisherman brought, we have never seen at all [kabisa].

NEGATIVE TENSES [N CLASS].

The Negative prefixes referring to Nouns

of the *n* class are *hai-* in the singular and *hazi-* in the plural.

> Nyumba yangu haikuanguka, *my house did not fall down.*
> Nyumba zile mbovu hazijaanguka bado, *those decayed houses have not fallen down as yet.*
> Sindano zetu hazingalivunjika, *our needles would not have been broken.*

Translate into Swahili.

All the money would not have been spent. His accounts did not please me. This profit will not suffice you. This air will not cure you. Their alms would not have pleased God. The chief's anger does not harm me. The sound of the bell did not annoy me. The roof beams did not rot. The canoe has not yet sunk. The clock is not striking. The clocks have not yet struck. The letter does not arrive. Your (pl.) letters did not arrive. The screw is not entering. The nose does not see.

THE U- CLASS.

Nouns which begin in the singular with U make their plural by changing U into N.

This rule is, however, subject to many exceptions and modifications.

1. U- before a vowel becomes W-.

> Wembe, *a razor.*
> Wino, *ink.*

2. Where the root of the noun begins with

a vowel the U- of the singular becomes Ny- in the plural.

 Uimbo, *a song.*   Nyimbo, *songs.*

3. Where the noun in the singular is a dissyllable the U- is retained and Ny- prefixed.

 Uma, *a fork.*   Nyuma, *forks.*

4. The letter N changes and is changed as mentioned above, p. 78.

The list of Substantives is not numerous, and many, being abstract nouns, have no plural. In the following list the plurals are added when in use.

List of Substantives of the U- class.

Ukubali, *acceptance.*
Uzee, *old age.*
Udevu, *a hair of the beard* — ndevu, *beard.*
Uzuri, *beauty.*
Uchungu, *bitterness.*
Upofu, *blindness.*
Upindi, *a bow* — pindi.
Upana, *breadth.*
Ukingo, *brink.*
Ufagio, *a broom* — fagio.
Utoto, *childhood.*
Ukucha, *a claw, a nail* — kucha.
Ushujaa, *courage, heroism.*
Ua, *a court yard* — nyua.
Wokovu, *deliverance.*
Umande, *dew.*
Uovu, *evil.*
Uso, *face* — nyuso.

THE U CLASS.

Uwongo, *falsehood.*
Uoga, *fear.*
Ukali, *fierceness.*
Ukuni, *a piece of firewood* — kuni, *firewood.*
Unga, *flour.*
Uayo, *foot print* — nyayo.
Uma, *a fork, sting* — nyuma.
Upole, *gentleness.*
Wema, *goodness, kindness.*
Wali, *cooked grain.*
Uji, *gruel.*
Ufizi, *gum of the teeth* — fizi.
Unyele, *a hair* — nyele, *the hair.*
Ukufi, *handful* — kufi.
Uwingu, *heaven* — mbingu.
Uvivu, *idleness.*
Urithi, *inheritance.*
Wino, *ink.*
Upele, *large pimples, itch.*
Ubishi, *joke.*
Ufunguo, *a key* — funguo.
Ufalme, *kingdom, kingship.*
Utambi, *a lamp wick* — tambi.
Ukurasa, *leaf of a book* — kurasa.
Urefu, *length.*
Umeme, *lightning.*
Unyonge, *meanness.*
Wavu, *a net used in hunting* — nyavu.
Usiku, *night.*
Upuuzi, *nonsense, silly talk.*
Uapo, *an oath* — nyapo.
Ubau, *a plank* — mbau.
Wingi, *plenty.*
Upondo, *a pole for punting* — pondo.
Ugali, *porridge.*

THE U CLASS.

Umasikini, poverty.
Uwezo, power, ability.
Ugomvi, a quarrel.
Utulivu, quietness.
Wembe, razor — nyembe.
Ufufuo, resurrection.
Wali, rice [when cooked].
Usabi, smallfly.
Utumwa, service, slavery, something which has to be done.
Usharika, sharing, partnership.
Unafi, shavings of wood, &c.
Werevu, shrewdness.
Ugonjwa, sickness, disease.
Upande, a side — pande.
Uimbo, a song — nyimbo.
Wengo, the spleen.
Usi, string, thread — nyuzi.
Ushi, a string course — nyushi.
Utepe, a stripe, a line — tepe.
Usultani, sultanship.
Upanga, a sword — panga.
Ukwaju, tamarinds.
Ukoga, tartar on the teeth.
Wasio, testament, judgment.
Uizi, theft, thievishness.
Wakati, time, season.
Ulimi, the tongue — ndimi.
Uthia, trouble, noise, confusion.
Uwaziri, visiership.
Ukuta, a wall — kuta.
Upotevu, wastefulness.
Uthaifu, weakness.
Utajiri, wealthiness.
Weupe, whiteness.

Utambi, *wick of a lamp* — tambi.
Upepo, *wind* — pepo.
Uchawi, *witchcraft*.
Ulimwengu, *the world*.
Ujana, *youth*.

ADJECTIVES [U CLASS].

Adjectives, including the variable numerals, are made to agree with substantives of the U class, when in the singular number, by prefixing m-, mu-, or mw-, as if agreeing with substantives of the class containing *mti*, a tree. See pp. 4 and 24.

  Wembe mkali, *a sharp razor*.
  Uimbo mwema, *a good song*.

Adjectives are made to agree with substantives of the U class, when in the plural number, by prefixing n- or ny-, as if agreeing with substantives of the N class. See p. 84.

  Funguo nzito, *heavy keys*.
  Nyembe kali, *sharp razors*.
  Nyimbo njema, *good songs*.

Translate into Swahili.

A great (much) age. A long beard. A long hair of the beard. Much beauty. A long bow. Long bows. Small brooms. Short claws. A long nail. A wide court-yard. Much dew. A fine face. Fine faces. A little piece of firewood. Dry firewood. White four. Soft flour. Many footprints. Red hair. A white hair. A thick hair. Black ink. Small keys. A thick lamp wick.

Thick planks. A light plank. Heavy punting poles. Two red planks. I want two long punting poles. I have bought five good planks. I heard three songs. I saw much flour. I remained one night.

PRONOUNS [U CLASS].

The pronominal syllables answering to the U class are *u* in the singular and *zi* in the plural. Thus—

Upole u mwema, *gentleness is good.*
Kuni zi fupi, *the firewood pieces are short.*
Urithi umepotea, *the inheritance is lost.*
Panga zimepotea, *the swords are lost.*
Nimeupata ufalme, *I have got the kingdom.*
Nimezitwaa funguo, *I have taken the keys.*

It will be observed that in the Pronouns as in Adjectives the singular forms are the same as those appropriate to Substantives like *mti*, a tree, and in the plural they are the same as those appropriate to plural Substantives of the n class. Thus—

Of is represented by *wa* and *za*.

The Possessive pronouns are formed by *w-* and *z-*.

The Demonstratives are *huu* and *hizi*.

The Interrogative *which?* becomes *upi?* and *zipi?*

Wembe wa Abdallah, *Abdallah's razor.*
Nyembe za Ali, *Ali's razors.*

PRONOUNS [U. CLASS].

Urefu wake, *its length.*
Mbau zake, *its planks.*

Wali huu, *this [cooked] rice.*
Funguo hizi, *these keys.*

Usiku upi, *which night?*
Fagio zipi, *which brooms?*

Unga wote, *all flour.*
Nyapo zote, *all oaths.*

The relatives referring to nouns of the *u* class are *wo* or *o* in the singular, and *zo* in the plural.

Ufunguo uliopotea, *the key which is lost.*
Funguo zilizopotea, *the keys which are lost.*
Utambi nilioukata, *the wick I cut.*
Tambi nilizozikata, *the wicks I cut.*
Ubishi wo wote, *any joke whatever.*

The negative prefixes used before a verb are *hau-* in the singular, and *hazi-* in the plural.

Ubau hautoshi, *the plank is not enough.*
Mbau hazitoshi, *the planks are not enough.*

Translate into Swahili.

The bow is broken. The sting hurts. The kingdom is prospering. I spilt the ink. The lightning struck a tree, and killed three men. The leaf of the book was brought, and it was torn. A plank was not wanted of great [much] length. The boy cut [some] firewood and hurt his face. They found the wicks and they were very short. The kingdom was conquered. The footprints are not visible. The fierceness of the chief annoys his people. The child took the keys and rubbed them. The joke pleased them. A handful of flour will suffice. The world is evil. This inheritance is not large. I held your sword. He picked up my razor, and brought it. The court yard was swept. The broom was lost. The hunting nets were broken, and the animals escaped. The idleness of the boy surprises me. This razor is sharp. This plank is short. This great kingdom. These songs. That cooked grain. Those brooms. Which bows? Yonder wide court yard. Those keys were lost. They have broken all those punting poles. That beautiful face. This bad flour. This footprint. That sharp sword.

The nonsense which you are talking. Those swords which I bought. He bought those forks which I refused. The walls which I built fell. All night the people danced and made a great [much] noise. I have picked up the keys which the child rubbed. He begged a handful of dates and I refused. I did not like his meanness when they wanted him to give [toa] (some) cooked grain, which he had cooked. They would not have brought the flour which I wanted.

THE -NI CASE.

All Substantives in Swahili (except the names of persons and animals) may be put into what may be called the locative case by suffixing -*ni*. The accent of the word is shifted by the suffix.

> Nyumba *becomes* nyumbáni.
> Mkunazi *becomes* mkunazíni.

THE -NI CASE.

The locative case expresses merely some relation of a local character, and may be translated by *in, to, at, from, out of, into, before, by,* or any other preposition in English expressing position. It has very nearly the same effect as the preposition *katika.*

It is rarely or never used with a noun followed by an adjective.

When the substantive is followed by a pronoun the pronoun may take one of three prefixes, *mw-, pa-, kw-,* and no other.

Mw- is used where the idea intended is that of locality *within.*

Nyumbani mwangu, *into* or *within my house.*

Pa- is used where the idea of nearness is intended.

Nyumbani pangu, *at, by, near,* or *before my house.*

Kw- is used where motion is the principal idea and in cases of distant objects, or where the idea is of an indefinite character. It is the most usual of the three prefixes.

Nyumbani kwangu, *to my house.*

Kwangu, kwako, &c., are used by themselves to express *at home, with me, you, &c., in my country, to my mind,* and so forth.

Translate into Swahili.

The man went into the stream [river]. And they followed into his house. They saw many trees in the garden. He pushed me until we arrived at our house. You know the date tree before my door. He slept with his book under his arm [in the armpit]. I have not yet returned to my town. I will wait under the tree in the road. He got out of the well and arrived (at) the town. He held his bow and his arrows in his hand. And they ran away, and hid themselves, in their house. When they arrived at the river, the people in the road laughed, and the donkey feared, kicked, and fell into the river and sank, and the man and the youth returned to their house.

INDECLINABLE ADJECTIVES.

The paucity of regular Adjectives is supplied in part by the use of words, borrowed chiefly from the Arabic, which have no prefixes, and therefore cannot vary according to the forms of their substantives. Such are—

Bora, *best, superior, preferable, great.*
Yakini, *certain.*
Rahisi, *cheap, easy.*
Safi, *clean, pure.*
Hodari, *clever, able, strong.*
Kamili, *complete, perfect, even (not odd).*
Rathi, *content.*
Sahihi, *correct, free from error.*
Fasihi, *correct, free from impropriety.*
Ghali, *dear, expensive.*
Yabis, *dry, solid.*
Killa, *every.*
Amini, *faithful, trustworthy.*
Haba, *few, too little.*

102 INDECLINABLE ADJECTIVES.

Imara, *firm.*
Huru, *free, not enslaved.*
Hafifu, *light, insignificant.*
Utupu, *naked.*
Halali, *lawful.*
Farathi, *obligatory, unavoidable.*
Kanuni, *indispensable, a necessary condition.*
Sunne, *advisable, recommended.*
Lazimu, *binding upon, compulsory.*
Haramu, *forbidden, unlawful.*
Thahiri, *manifest, evident, clear.*
Kadiri, *moderate, middling.*
Tele, *plenty, a good deal of.*
Marithawa, *plenty, abundant.*
Masikini, *poor.*
Tayari, *ready.*
Salama, *safe, not hurt.*
Laini, *smooth, soft, gentle.*
Thaifu, *weak, inferior, good for nothing.*

Killa stands alone in always preceding its substantives.

Killa siku, *every day.*

Translate into Swahili.

You (are) good for nothing. His house (is) clean. Those eggs (are) cheap. His slaves (are) faithful. Every man carried a sword. The books (are) dear. The wood which you bought (is) smooth. These children (are) content with their good food. Those men (are) not slaves, they (are) free. The boxes which they are making (are) ready. Their punting poles are complete. Your misfortunes (are) light. My work (is) inferior. Your work (is) superior. They sent too little lime. The church which they are building is firm. It is not lawful to kill. That strong man who is fighting will conquer the weak (man). The bananas in their garden (are) abundant. The food which they are refusing (is) dry. All those people are poor. I found him naked.

COMPOUND ADJECTIVES.

Substantives and Verbs may be converted into Adjectives by prefixing the variable particle -*a*.

Mtu wa akili, a sensible man, a man of sense.
Nyumba ya kupendeza, a pleasing house.
Mbau za kutosha, planks enough.

Adjectives of this kind may be made as they are wanted. The following are a few of the most useful.

Ancient, -a kale.
Civilised, -a kiungwana.
Cold, -a baridi.
Crafty, -a hila.
Dark (not light), -a giza.
Eternal, -a milele.
European, -a kizungu.
First, former, -a kwanza.
Fortunate, -a bahati, -a heri.
Hot (of things), -a moto.
Human, -a mwana Adamu.
Just, -a haki.
Left hand, -a kushoto.
The other, -a pili.
Other people's, -a watu.

COMPOUND ADJECTIVES.

Regular, -a kaida.
Right hand, -a kulia, -a kuume.
Round, -a mviringo.
Secret, -a siri.
Some one else's, -a mwenyewe.
True, -a kweli.
Uncivilized, -a kishenzi.
Valuable, -a thamani.
Wild, -a mwituni.

The ordinal numbers are formed on the same system.

First, -a kwanza *or* -a mosi.
Second, -a pili.
Third, -a tatu.
Fourth, -a 'nne.
Fifth, -a tatu.
Sixth, -a sita.
Seventh, -a saba.
Eighth, -a nane.
Ninth, -a tisa, -a tissia, -a kenda.
Tenth, -a kumi.
Eleventh, -a edashara.
Twelfth, -a thenashara.
Twentieth, -a asharini.
Hundredth, -a mia.
Last, -a mwisho.

Translate into Swahili.

These books (are) ancient. He does not know civilized customs. After the time of the rains the cold winds begin (anza). Crafty people are often deceived. Little work is done (in the) dark days. Very bad circumstances are not eternal. European cloth is dear. They burnt down the first town which they conquered. The fortunate man has bought a pleasing house. He spilt the hot coffee. A just man is loved by his slave. Our custom (is) to pass on the left side of the road. The sensible man refused to remain in the other house. They cooked his porridge in somebody else's cooking pot. Don't put on other people's clothes. The right hand wall of the house fell. He himself built a round hut. The Sultan (Sultani) is considering the secret affairs of his kingdom. The uncivilized chief destroyed the valuable book. Call the second man. Cut down every fourth tree. The ninth house fell down. I will pay you every tenth day.

ADJECTIVAL VERBS.

A large part of the work of English Adjectives is done in Swahili by Verbs, which denote the possessing or rather acquiring the quality. The -me- tense as a rule denotes the present possessing of the quality, and therefore answers to the English present with *is* or *are*. The relative past tense with -*li*- forms a quasi adjective, and the negative relative a corresponding privative adjective.

  Mtungi unajaa, *the water jar is getting full.*
  Mtungi umejaa, *the water jar is full.*
  Mtungi uliojaa, *the full water jar.*
  Mtungi usiojaa, *the not full water jar.*
   Kitu kilichopotea, *the lost thing.*
   Kitu kisichopotea, *the thing not lost.*

ADJECTIVAL VERBS.

Neno lililopendeza, *the pleasing word.*
Neno lisilopendeza, *the unpleasing word.*

To become audible, kusikiliana.
    blind, kupofuka.
    well boiled, kutokoseka.
    broken, kuvunjika.
    bright (by rubbing), kukatuka.
        (shining), kung'ara.
    bruised, kuchubuka.
    callous, kufaganzi.
    carved, kunakishiwa.
    cheap, kurahisika.
    clean, kutakata, kutakasika.
    clear (of the sky), kutakata.
        (manifest), kuelea.
    comforted, kufarajika.
    comfortable, kutengenea.
    complete, kutimia.
    confident, kutumaini.
    confused, kufathaika.
    crooked, kupotoka.
    in disorder, kuchafuka.
    dry, kukauka.
    enough, kutosha.
    fat, kunona.
    fatigued, kuchoka.
    flexible, kupindana.
    flourishing, kusitawi.
    foolish, kupumbazika.
    full, kujaa.
        (with eating), kushiba.
    full grown, kukomaa, kupevuka.
    heavy to, kulemea.
    humble, kunenyekea.
    intoxicated, kulewa.

ADJECTIVAL VERBS.

To become lean, kukonda.
    less, kupunguka.
    loose, kulegea.
    mouldy, kufanya ukungu.
    more, kuzidi.
    obligatory upon, kulazimu.
    open, kufunuka.
    opposite, kuelekea.
    paralytic, kupooza.
    patient, kuvumilia, kustahimili.
    perfect, kukamilika.
    pleasing, kupendeza.
    precipitous, kuchongoka.
    putrid, kuoza.
    quiet, kutulia.
    rough, kuparuza.
    round, kuviringa.
    scorched, or scalded, kuungua.
    sick, kuugua.
    silent, kunyamaza.
    sober, kulevuka.
    sorry, kusikitika.
    spherical, kuviringana.
    stunted, kuvia.
    tangled, kutatana.
    tight, kukazana.
    torn, kupasuka.
    uncomfortable (of persons), kusumbuka.
    unsewn, kufumuka.
    useful to, kufaa.
    visible, kuonekana.
    void, kutanguka.
    weak, kuthoofika.
    weary, kuchoka.
    well, kupona.

ADJECTIVAL VERBS.

To become wrinkled, kukunjana.

Translate into Swahili.

The man's voice is audible. The children became blind. The well boiled eggs. The broken water-jars. The children's keys are bright. The moon is brilliant. The child's leg is bruised. The knee is callous. The door is carved. The food became cheap. The spoons will not be clean. The heavens are clear. Your words are clear. Your soul is comforted. You are extremely comfortable. The bow is flexible. He is confident. You are confused. The rope is crooked. The child is well. The room is in disorder. The road is dry. The food is enough. The slaves were fatigued. Our work is flourishing. The overseer was sober. The trees are stunted. The thread is tangled. His waistcoat is tight. Abdallah is uncomfortable. The bag is unsewn. He is useful. The agreement is void. The youth is weak. Majaliwa is weary with work. The old man is wrinkled. A wrinkled face. The pearl is useful to me. A stunted tree. I am not at all sorry. A silent slave girl. A scalded child dreads the fire. The world is spherical. A round box. A rough road. A quiet youth. Putrid meat. A precipitous rock. The pleasing overseer. The number is perfect. A paralytic old man. The dhow is opposite to our home. The flower is open. My hunger has become more. The mouldy loaf. My hunger has become less. The intoxicated slaves. Humble Europeans. The load has become heavy to the porter. The bananas are full grown. The foreigner is becoming foolish.

RELATIVE WITHOUT NOTE OF TIME.

The Relative may be connected with a Verb without any tense prefix, which then has something of the nature of an Adjective, or Adjectival Substantive.

The sign of the person must precede and the sign of the Relative follow the Verb. An objective prefix may be inserted between the personal prefix and the Verb.

Umpendaye, *whom you love = your beloved,* or *(you) who love him = you his lover.*
Niwezaye, [*I*] *who can.*
Warukao, *they which fly = flying things.*
Asikiaye, *he who hears = a hearer.*
Nipitayo, *you who pass = ye passers by.*
Kiviringacho, *which is rounded = round.*

Translate into Swahili.

The person you love has come back. The chief you fear has got well. The fire which burns in my house will cook the meat you bring. You will get all the food I cook in your cooking pot. The books you read will not be of use to you. You will find the profit you look for. The door I open I shall not shut.

NAMES OF ANIMALS.

Names of animals and living things generally are constructed with adjectives and pronouns proper to the first class.

>Mtu mzuri, *a fine man.*
>Ng'ombe mzuri, *a fine ox.*
>Kiboko mzuri, *a fine hippopotamus.*
>Sultani mzuri, *a fine sultan.*

>Watu wazuri, *fine people.*
>Ng'ombe wazuri, *fine oxen.*
>Viboko wazuri, *fine hippopotamus.*
>Masultani wazuri, *fine sultans.*

Titles of office, being foreign words, are made plural by prefixing *ma-*.

>Waziri, *a vizier.*   Mawaziri, *viziers.*

List of names of Persons, Animals, &c. The plural is added in each case.

Habeshia, *Abyssinian,* mahabeshia.
Wakili, *agent,* mawakili.
Nyama, *animal,* nyama.
Siafu, *biting ants,* siafu.
Chungu, *ants,* chungu.
Mchwa, *white ants,* mchwa.
Nyani, *ape,* nyani.
Punda, *ass, donkey,* punda.
Shangazi, *aunt,* mashangazi.
Kinyozi, *barber,* vinyozi.
Nyuki, *bee,* nyuki.
Ndege, *bird,* ndege.

NAMES OF ANIMALS. 111

Kipofu, *a blind person*, vipofu.
Kijana, *boy or girl*, vijana.
Ndugu, *brother or sister*, ndugu.
Nyati, *buffalo*, nyati.
Fahali, *bull*, mafahali.
Ngamia, *camel*, ngamia.
Sermala, *carpenter*, masermala.
Paka, *cat*, paka.
Ng'ombe, *cattle, cow, ox*, ng'ombe.
Taandu, *centipede*, taandu.
Jumbe, *chief*, majumbe.
Jogoo, *cock*, majogoo.
Mende, *cockroach*, mende.
Jemadari, *commander*, majemadari.
Suria, *concubine*, masuria.
Mamba, *crocodile*, mamba.
Kiziwi, *a deaf person*, viziwi.
Mbwa, *dog*, mbwa.
Bata, *duck*, mabata.
Kibeti, *dwarf*, vibeti.
Tembo, *elephant*, tembo.
Adui, *enemy*, maadui, *or* adui.
Baba, *father*, baba.
Samaki, *fish*, samaki.
Kiroboto, *flea*, viroboto.
Inzi, *fly*, mainzi.
Kuku, *fowl, hen*, kuku.
Rafiki, *friend*, marafiki.
Chura, *frog*, vyura.
Paa, *gazelle*, paa.
Kijakazi, *slave girl*, vijakazi.
Mbuzi, *goat*, mbuzi.
Liwali, *governor*, maliwali.
Bibi, *grandmother*, bibi.
Mwewe, *hawk*, mwewe.

NAMES OF ANIMALS.

Kiboko, *hippopotamus*, viboko.
Frasi, *horse*, frasi.
Banyani, *heathen Indian*, Mabanyani.
Jini, *a jin, a spirit*, majini.
Kathi, *judge*, makathi.
Bibi, *lady, mistress*, bibi.
Chui, *leopard*, chui.
Simba, *lion*, simba.
Bwana, *master*, bwana.
Kima, *monkey*, kima.
Mama, *mother*, mama.
Nguruwe, *pig*, nguruwe.
Njiwa, *pigeon*, njiwa.
Kasisi, *Christian priest*, makasisi.
Sungura, *rabbit*, sungura.
Panya, *rat*, panya.
Kifaru, *rhinoceros*, vifarn.
Baharia, *sailor*, baharia.
Nge, *scorpion*, nge.
Papa, *shark*, papa.
Kondoo, *sheep*, kondoo.
Nyoka, *snake*, nyoka.
Asikari, *soldier*, asikari.
Kobe, *tortoise*, kobe.
Kasa, *turtle*, kasa.
Hua, *turtle dove*, hua.
Dobi, *washerman*, dobi.
Punda milia, *zebra*, punda milia.

Translate into Swahili.

I told the soldiers, and they called the commander. The tall Abyssinian told the fierce agent. The great elephant was bitten by ants. The white ants [are] our enemies. The large apes are in the

NAMES OF ANIMALS.

trees. The barber's white donkey kicked my aunt. The bees make honey. The boys saw a camel, their sister saw two fine birds. The carpenter was stung by a centipede. I saw the chief; he bought many cattle, and many cocks and hens, and large ducks. I saw a dog; he was bitten by the flies. My friends do not like the cockroaches. The slave girl has bought a beautiful gazelle. My father bought much fruit (pl.); a dwarf his enemy took it. The lady was afraid of the large frogs; the master said, The great lion and the fierce leopard are feared, but people of understanding do not fear a frog. The jin bewitched [made witchcraft against] the governor; his mother wanted to kill a large pig and three pigeons; the Christian priest told her this (haya) [was] nonsense. When the sailor was bathing, I saw a shark come (it came) and seize (and it seized) him with its teeth. I bought eight fat sheep. The cunning snake suddenly took the rabbit. The washerman bought a donkey, but the soldiers got it; and [hatta] as they were taking it away [chukua] a scorpion stung it [on] the foot. The good judge passed [by] and saw the soldiers; he ordered them to be beaten by the sailors of our Sultan's vessel.

Short blind men. A foreign deaf man. A large flea. Female hippopotamus. A whole rhinoceros. A beautiful slave girl. Beautiful youths. Eight jealous deaf people. Six heavy hippopotamus. Those fleas. These slave girls. That hippopotamus is fierce. The blind person is dead. Who is this blind person? Your slave girls took my umbrella. The oxen are fat. The donkeys were full. The lean ox.

COMPARISON OF ADJECTIVES.

There are no degrees of comparison in Swahili. The effect of the Superlative in English is generally given by the simple use of the adjective, as if in an absolute sense.

Huyu mwema.   *This (man is the) best.*
Yupi mwema?   *Which (man is the) best?*

Where the superlative is joined in English with a definite article, or a possessive pronoun, the relative is employed in Swahili.

The broadest road, *Njia iliyo pana.*
My sharpest sword, *Upanga wangu ulio mkali.*

If it is necessary to employ both the positive and the superlative, the latter may be distinguished by adding *sana*.

Huyu mwema, lakini aliye mwema sana ni huyu.
This man is good, but the best man (the man who is very good) is this.

The Comparative is expressed by the use of *kuliko*, where there is.

Huyu mwema kuliko yule, *this man is good where that man is, i.e., he is the good one (the better) of the two.*

Saa hii njema kuliko ile, *This watch is better than that.*

Translate into Swahili.

Malindi (Melinda) is a more ancient town than Mvita (Mombas). The language of the people of Mvita is more correct than the language of Unguja (Zanzibar). Bad people [are] worse than animals. Date trees [are] more beautiful than cocoanut trees. The bitterest medicine. This woollen cloth is blacker than this, but the blackest is that yonder. This river is broader than the Rovuma. Is that place cleaner than this? My joy is more complete than yours. The overlooker's accounts are more correct than those of the fisherman. The slaves [were] more cunning than the overlooker, and they deceived him. The European [was] more fierce than the mason, and beat all the slaves. The gunpowder in the barrel [is] drier than the soap, which [is] in this box. This pole is firmer than that which was put into the pit yesterday. This waterjar is fuller than that. Abdallah's house is larger than mine, but mine is more beautiful than all the houses which I have seen. This road is longer than that to your house, but the shortest passes by your plantation. Which wood [is] hardest? The chief [is] weaker than the thieves. A piece of firewood is lighter than a thick plank. These bananas are redder and more sweet than yours. Our smallest bell is heavier than their largest. Abdallah bin Ali's beard is long, but Suleman's is the longest [that of Suleman long very].

TO BE.

In Swahili the present tense of the Verb *to be* may be rendered in eight different ways.

1. By simple omission.

    Nyumba hii kubwa, *this house is large.*

2. By *ni* for all persons and both numbers.

Bwana wangu ni Sultani, *my master is the Sultan*.

3. By the sign of the person.

Tu tayari, *we are ready*.

4, 5, and 6. By the sign of the person followed by the syllables -ko, -mo, and -po.

Bwana yumo nyumbani, *master is inside the house*.
Bithaa nyingi ziko kwangu, *much merchandise is at my house*.
Yupo hapa msimamizi, *the overlooker is here*.

7. By the sign of the person followed by -na.

Kuna mtu, *there is a man*.

8. By the syllable -li- inserted between the sign of the person and a relative particle.

Aliye, *(he) who is*.
Zilizo, *(those) which are*.

Of these the three most important are, 1. By omission, which is customary wherever the verb *to be* is used as a mere connective. 5. By the personal sign followed by -ko, which must be used when *being in a place* is intended, and is the usual form where the verb *to be* stands alone, or without any substantive or adjective immediately following it. 8. By -li- with a relative. The other uses will be found explained in the grammar, but they will be little wanted by a beginner.

TO BE. 117

It is unnecessary to give any further exercises on the first rule.

Translate into Swahili.

The book is on the table. The cook is near. The planks are in the ship. The fishermen are by the canoe. The canoes are on the water. The carts are on the road. The oranges are in the basket. Are there many slaves in your town? There are [they are]. I saw six ships yesterday, where are they now? They are by the island. Are there [are they] canoes near them? There are seven canoes very near. Where is our overlooker? He is at the plantation. Are there slaves with him? There are twenty. Who is (there)? Abdallah is (there). Where is Ali? He is at the house. The chief is outside.

I who am good. You who are bad. He who is weak. She who is idle. We who are gentle. You (pl.) who are fierce. A stone which is large. A house which is small. Dates which are sweet. A man who is an old man. A chief who is a drunkard. A piece which is little. A chest which is heavy. Arrows which are sharp. Goods (merchandise) which are dear.

Where locality is part of the idea, the particle -ko is added after the relative.

Watu walioko chini, *the people who are below.*

Translate into Swahili.

The book which is on the table. The planks which are in the ship. The fishermen who are by the canoe. The canoes which are on the water. The oranges which are on the trees. The slaves which are in our town will all run away, when they see the gun which is in your hand. The ships which are by the island will destroy the town which is (on) this side of the river. The chief who is in our town. The trees which are by the road.

The past tense *was, where, had been*, is expressed by -likuwa or -alikuwa with the proper prefix. It is followed by -ko when *being in a place* is part of the idea intended.

Nalikuwa, *I was*.
Walikuwa, *you were, thou wast*.
Alikuwa, *he or she was*.
Walikuwa, Yalikuwa, Chalikuwa, Lalikuwa, Palikuwa, *it was*.
Twalikuwa, *we were*.
Mwalikuwa, *you were*.
Walikuwa, Yalikuwa, Zalikuwa, Vyalikuwa, *they were*.
Alikuwako, *he was (there)*.

Translate into Swahili.

Abdallah was chief, I was a slave. You were a good man. He was a fisherman. They were idle slaves. The Europeans were fierce people. Those people were all black. The owner was a man of sense, the others were simpletons.

The black men were in the forest. The European was by the cannon. The gun was in the house. The house was by the river, the river was near the mountain. The mountain was in the island. The island was in the sea. Many people were in the town, but few people were outside the houses.

The relative particles are used in the ordinary way with this past tense, and the particle *ko* is added when required.

Niliyekuwa(ko), (*I*) *who was*.
Uliyekuwa(ko), (*you*) *who were*.
Aliyekuwa(ko), (*He or she*) *who was*.
Uliokuwa(ko), Iliyokuwa(ko), Kilichokuwa(ko), Lililokuwa(ko), Palipokuwa(ko), (*it*) *which was*.
Tuliokuwa(ko), (*we*) *who were*.
Mliokuwa(ko), (*you*) *who were*.
Waliokuwa(ko), (*they*) *who were*.
Iliyokuwa(ko), Zilizokuwa(ko), Vilivyokuwa(ko), Yaliyokuwa(ko), (*they*) *which were*.

Translate into Swahili.

The chief was in the house, his people were [there] far off. The European was on the top of the rock. The canoe was near. I saw two men who were at the door of the house near the date tree. The chief said you were an old man long ago, and I said to him, were you a child? And he said to me, I was a youth. The ships were on the sea, the men were in the town. The slaves were the European's servants. I was in the town, and I saw the ancient houses which were there. I saw many people, they were on the road, but those whom our companions saw were in the wood and they (were) few. Many people were with the chief. A few ran away, those who ran away were afterwards in our town, and I killed them all. Five large chests were in my house many days.

The men who were in the town were afraid, we who were outside ran away. The chief called the fishermen, who were by the canoe. Did you see the people who were (there)? How many canoes which were (there) have sunk? The European cut down all the trees which were on the plantation. The chief killed all who were our slaves. The chests which were at my house were broken by the thieves who were afterwards in your town. The houses which were (there) have all fallen down. I bought all the books which were (there). He brought the book which was on my table.

IRREGULAR VERBS.

The only really irregular form in Swahili is the Imperative of the Verb *kuja*, to come, which makes *njoo* and *njooni*, come and come ye. Monosyllabic verbs, however, and dissyllabic verbs beginning with a vowel keep the *ku-* of the Infinitive in many of their tenses, and thus are apparently irregular. The following table of the tenses of the verb *to come* will show the cases in which the *ku-* is retained.

Naja, I come.
Nikaja, and I came.
Nikija, I coming.
Siji, I come not.
Sikuja, I did not come.
Sijaja, I am not yet come.
Nisije, let me not come.
Nije, let me come.
Nijaye, I who come.

IRREGULAR VERBS. 121

Ninakuja, I am coming.
Nimekuja, I have come.
Nalikuja, I came.
Nitakuja, I shall come.
Nijapokuja, even if I come.
Ningekuja, I should come.
Ningalikuja, I should have come.
Nisijekuja, before I come.
Nisipokuja, when I come not.
Niliyekuja, I who came.

This irregularity depends upon the question of accent, as the insertion of an objective prefix makes it unnecessary. Thus—

Amekula, *he has eaten.*
Amemla, *he has eaten him.*

Kupa, to give to, must always have the objective prefix, and therefore is never irregular.

Nimempa, *I have given him.*
Atanipa, *he will give me.*

List of Monosyllabic Verbs.

Kucha, *to rise (of the sun), to fear.*
  chwa *or* twa, *to set (of the sun), to be feared.*
  fa, *to die.*
  ja, *to come.*
  la, *to eat.*
  nya, *to fall like rain, to rain.*
  nywa *or* nwa, *to drink.*
  pa, *to give to.*
  wa, *to be, to become.*

The passives, *kuliwa,* to be eaten, *kunyewa,* to be drunk up, *kupewa,* to receive, are regular.

Dissyllable Vowel Verbs.

Kuanza, *to begin.*
  enda, *to go.*
  iba, *to steal.*
  imba, *to sing.*
  isha, *to finish, to come to an end.*
  ita, *to call.*
  iva, *to get ripe.*
  oga, *to bathe* (*pronounced* koga).
  oka, *to bake.*
  uza, *to sell* (*pronounced* kuza).

Translate into Swahili.

The five thieves stole the chests which were at my house. The merchandise which was in the ship was stolen by the fishermen. The slave women began to sing. They sang many beautiful songs. The chief went to bathe in the river. The bananas are not yet ripe, they are full grown, but they are not sweet. You sold four slaves yourself. We will bake the bread (mikate), which you will want on the road. Our money is finished, we cannot buy your pumpkins. The mangoes will come to an end, if you eat them now. Who [is it who] called me? Who [is it who] is singing? I have not finished yet. When shall you come to an end? Do not steal people. Go (pl.) into the town, and call five people to sing songs at my house. Our people have eaten all the bananas, we have not sold even one. You will die. He will come to our home. We shall eat meat. The meat has been eaten, which he received from me (was given by me). Let us eat and drink. The night will come and the slaves will eat. We always drink water only. The sun is setting.

TO HAVE.

The verb to have is expressed in Swahili by *kuwa na,* to be with.

   Nina, *I have.*
   Una, *thou hast, you have.*
   Ana, *he or she has.*
Una, Ina, Kina, Lina, Pana, Kuna, *it has.*
   Tuna, *we have.*
   Mna, *ye have, you have.*
Wana, Ina, Zina, Vina, Yana, *they have.*
   Sina, *I have not.*
   Huna, *you have not.*
   Hana, *he or she has not.*
Hauna, Haina, Hakina, Halina, Hapana, Hakuna, *it has not.*
   Hatuna, *we have not.*
   Hamna, *ye have not.*
Hawana, Haina, Hazina, Havina, Hayana, *they have not.*
   Nalikuwa na, *I had.*
   Walikuwa na, *you had.*
   Alikuwa na, *he or she had.*
Walikuwa na, Yalikuwa na, Chalikuwa na, Lalikuwa na, Palikuwa na, Kulikuwa na, *it had.*
   Twalikuwa na, *we had.*
   Mwalikuwa na, *ye had.*
Walikuwa na, Yalikuwa na, Zalikuwa na, Vyalikuwa na, *they had.*

TO HAVE.

Nitakuwa na, &c., *I, &c., shall have.*

The other tenses are formed in the same manner. Where an objective prefix would be used with an ordinary verb, the relative particle is added to the final *na* (p. 34).

Ninalo, *I have it* (kasha).
Ninazo, *I have them* (nyumba).
Nalikuwa nazo nyumba hizi, *I had these houses.*
Sikuwa na kisu, kama ningalikuwa nacho ningalimua, *I had no knife, if I had had one, I should have killed him.*

When joined with a relative, the relative particle attaches itself to the verb *kuwa*, and so occurs twice.

Kasha nililo nalo, *the chest I have, i.e., which I am with it.*
Kitu cho chote alicho nacho, *anything whatever which he has.*
Fetha nilizokuwa nazo, *the money I had.*

Translate into Swahili.

I wanted to buy all the cocoanuts which the chief had, but I find he had many which I did not get. I have a sword and (you) you have a spear and a shield, what are we to fear? If a man has money he will be great. If a man has not money he will not be great. My house is large, it has not a door. I had not a house formerly, now I have these three. The thieves stole every thing which we had. The old man has many valuable books. I shall buy all the books the Europeans have. I sold all the books I had myself, except those which you gave me. I have them now at [my] house. If Abdallah dies, I shall have much money. I shall have the property which you will give me. If you give me nothing (if you give me not anything), I shall have nothing. He tried to kill me and I struck him with a sword I had.

The same form of verb which signifies *to have* signifies also *to be* in the sense of *to exist*. It occurs most commonly in the words *hakuna* and *hapana*, there is not.

  Kuna mtu, *there is somebody.*
  Hakuna mtu, *there is nobody.*
  Hapana mtu, *nobody is there.*
Kulikuwa (*or* Palikuwa) na mtu, *there was a man.*

Translate into Swahili.

There is nobody in the house. There is nobody who knows (how) to conquer him. There is nothing outside. I sought for a knife, but there is no knife. I saw a sword in his hand, I looked again and he had no sword, even now there is none. There was somebody, now there is nobody.

COMPOUND TENSES.

The Verb *to be* is used in Swahili to form compound tenses in a manner very similar to that in which it is used in English. The verb *to have* is not used as an auxiliary in Swahili.

The present and past Participles in English are represented in Swahili by the ki and me tenses.

  Nalikuwa nikitoka, *I was going out.*
  Nalikuwa nimetoka, *I was gone out.*

COMPOUND TENSES.

The most useful compound tenses are the past imperfect, the future of a continuing action, and the pluperfect.

Nalikuwa nikienda, *I was going*.
Nitakuwa nikienda, *I shall be on my way*.
Nalikuwa nimekwenda, *I had gone*.
Sikuwa nikija, *I was not coming*.

The verb *kuisha* or *kwisha* is very commonly used to give emphasis to a past or perfect tense.

Amekwisha kuja, *he has finished to come, he is come already, he is certainly come.*

Translate into Swahili.

I was not going to the town, but shall go back now. He was eating. I did not see him, he had passed already. The thief had stolen some money. Had you read the book? I had not read it. I was looking at it. The fishermen were on the sea, they had found a few fishes [in] the night. The boys were cultivating their plantation. He had fastened the door. I had cut their fingers. I shall be cutting down their date trees. He was eating his food. He has done eating. They were stealing cocoanuts at my shamba. The slaves were telling me all the news of the thieves. The overlooker was going, but the slave girls had run away. I shall be going out from the house. He was entering at the door. I saw you, you were boxing my slave boy's ears.

DERIVATIVE VERBS.

A Verb in Swahili may be made causative, neuter, or reciprocal, by a change in its termination. Another change supplies the place of an English preposition. Thus *kuleta* is *to bring*, but *bring to me* is not expressed by *leta kwa mimi*, the proper expression is *niletea*; the -e- inserted before the final -a takes the place of the preposition *to*, as it would equally well that of any other. In the simple form the thing brought is the object of the verb, in the prepositional or applied form the person to, for, &c., whom it is brought is the object of the verb. Consequently in the passive *kuletwa* means *to be brought*, *kuletewa*, *to be brought to*, i.e., *to have brought to one*.

Waraka umeletwa, *a letter has been brought*.
Nimeletewa waraka, *I have had a letter brought me*.

The vowel inserted before the final -a is -e- if the vowel of the verb immediately preceding is -o- or -e-.

What are the applied forms of—

Kuomba. Kuoga. Kuleta. Kujenga. Kuseta. Kuponya. Kukokota. Kuota. Kueleza. Kuona. Kutoka. Kuondoka. Kutweka. Kucheka. Kulegeza. Kukosa. Kuweka. Kusema. Kupeleka. Kunena. Kungoja. Kuosha. Kuenda.

Translate into Swahili.

He prayed for me. I brought him the book.

They built us a wall. I will cure your slave for you. I dreamed about the chief. The old man explained to us the sound we had heard. I see evil for you. A place we shall go out at. I rose to him. We hoisted a flag for the chief. The cook put away much food for the children. I waited upon him many days. Wash these plates for me. He went by this road.

The vowel inserted before the final -a is -i- when the preceding vowel is -a-, -i-, or -u-.

Kufanya, *to make*.
Kufanyia, *to make for, out of, &c.*

What are the applied forms of—

Kupiga. Kufika. Kuuliza. Kuamka. Kuuma. Kuvunja. Kuita. Kukamata. Kugeuka. Kupanda. Kukusanya. Kuvuka. Kulima. Kukata. Kulinda. Kukana. Kuchimba. Kuvuta. Kufukuza. Kumwaga. Kupunguka. Kuisha. Kukunja. Kupata. Kushuka. Kufisha. Kuacha. Kutazama. Kutafuta. Kupima. Kulipa. Kuimba. Kusikitika. Kusimama. Kutupa. Kufunga. Kufuta.

Translate into Swahili.

I want you to beat this man for me. I shall ask about the cook. You have broken my knife for me. I do not know what I was called for. The net which you catch animals with. The caravan porters turned from me. They climbed up to me. The chief gathered all his people to them. I do not see the canoe they crossed in. We are cultivating for the chief. Cut me a stick. He denied to the chief

DERIVATIVE VERBS.

the words he hid from me. I shall not dig for you. Drive the slaves from us. The fishermen were looking for a ship. He refused to measure the road for me. The slave women were singing to the overlooker at your plantation and (he) he was paying money to them. I am sorry for you. Throw the spear at him. Fasten the door against them. The chief was sung to by our people. I was pelted (thrown stones at) by the youths. I had a plantation left to me. I was pitied (sikitikiwa).

Verbs which end in two vowels insert an -l- in making their applied form.

>Kufungua, *to unfasten*.
>>Kufungulia, *to unfasten to, or for, &c.*
>
>Kung'oa, *to root up*.
>>Kung'olea, *to root up for, with, &c.*

What are the applied forms of—

Kusumbua. Kuzaa. Kuchukua. Kuchagua. Kupangua. Kusikia. Kuzuia. Kuamua. Kulia. Kununua. Kupindua. Kutia. Kuvaa. Kutoa. Kupokea. Kukataa. Kukaa. Kusugua. Kukimbia. Kunyoa. Kupasua. Kutwaa. Kuvua. Kurarua. Kufunua. Kutembea.

The passives of these applied forms are often used as the passives of the simple verb.

>Kutwaliwa, *to be taken away, to have taken from one*.
>Kisu changu kimetwaliwa, *my knife has been taken*.
>Nimetwaliwa kisu changu, *I have had my knife taken from me*.

The reason for this use seems to lie in the difficulty of pronouncing the regular passive form.

Translate into Swahili.

Let us walk about the town. Unfasten the door for us. Uncover the pot for the cook. I took off my sandals in his honour (for him). They have taken from me my children. Give me an axe that I may split the planks with (it). Where (is) the razor I was shaved with? They want a city for them to flee to (it). Rub the table for us. The kings did not refuse to him his request. The first man received the money for the second. I have put out the money for you. The trees have all been pulled up. I have had all my trees pulled up. He was lifted up. The slave killed the animal for his chief. Unfasten the door for me.

Verbs in -e make their prepositional form in -ea.

    Kusamehe, *to forgive.*
    Kusamehea, *to forgive to.*

Verbs in -i and -u make their prepositional form in -ia.

    Kukubali, *to accept.*
    Kukubalia, *to accept for.*
    Kusifu, *to praise.*
    Kusifia, *to praise for.*

Verbs ending in -au make their prepositional forms in -aulia.

    Kusahau, *to forget.*
    Kusahaulia, *to forget in regard to.*

DERIVATIVE VERBS.

The passive of these prepositional forms is used as the passive of the simple verbs.

Kuharibiwa, *to be destroyed.*

What are the prepositional forms and passives of the following verbs—

Kubatili. Kushtaki. Kukubali. Kubadili. Kuhubiri. Kujibu. Kuwasili. Kuhimili. Kusihi. Kusadiki. Kuamini. Kujelidi. Kubariki. Kukirithi. Kuzabuni. Kutakabathi. Kudiriki. Kuathibu. Kuhitari. Kutahiri. Kushawishi. Kukaribu. Kufariji. Kuamuru. Kuhitimu. Kusetiri. Kukiri. Kutumaini. Kufikiri. Kusahihi. Kuwakifu. Kutamani. Kuhuluku. Kusulibi. Kuvinjari. Kulaani. Kuthubutu. Kufariki. Kuthalimu. Kufawiti. Kuhini. Kuuzulu. Kustahili. Kufathili. Kutharau. Kuasi. Kustarehe. Kuhusudu. Kutanafusi. Kuketi. Kustahimili. Kuhakiki. Kusayili. Kutahidi. Kufasiri. Kubaini. Kufurahi. Kusitawi. Kutabiri. Kubashiri. Kusahau. Kukabithi. Kunathiri. Kumiliki. Kuthani. Kuhami. Kuthuru. Kuauni. Kuarifu. Kuhifathi. Kurudi. Kutuhumu. Kugharimu. Kufuturu. Kusakifu. Kurissimu. Kuhalifu. Kukabili. Kusamehe. Kusubiri. Kudumu. Kulaabu. Kuabudu. Kuhutubu. Kuafu. Kukirihi. Kusujudu. Kufidi. Kutubu. Kushutumu. Kuhui. Kutilifu. Kukinai. Kufilisi. Kufitini. Kusaki. Kudai. Kuruzuku. Kuthamini. Kuhadithi. Kushuhudu. Kusafiri. Katadariki. Kujeruhi. Kustaajabu.

There are two uses of the applied form which should be remembered:—

132 DERIVATIVE VERBS.

1. Where something is described as serving a certain purpose, in Swahili the applied form of the verb is used preceded by the particle -a.

A knife to cut meat with, kisu cha kukatia nyama.
A place to go out at, mahali pa kutokea.

2. The applied form followed by *mbali* denotes that the thing is done fully and finally.

Afie mbali, *that he may die out of the way.*
Katupia mbali, *and throw it clean away.*

Translate into Swahili.

An axe to split firewood with. A word to answer him with. A stick to beat a dog with. A wind blew the papers clean away. The men want poles to build with. I see no man (I do not see a man) to call to. I have porters to carry for me. I see a place to climb up to. A pot to cook sweet potatoes in. They cut a mast away. The slaves have hoes to cultivate with. A rope to draw a cart with. The chief drove his enemies away altogether. I do not find words to explain my meaning with. Where is a chain to fasten him with? The birds flew away. Give me (some) long nails [msomari] to fasten the planks with. Let us kill them all out of the way. Push the stone away altogether. A bedstead to rest upon. Bring water to wash the plates with. I have a cloth to wipe them with afterwards.

RECIPROCAL VERBS.

Verbs are made reciprocal by changing the final -a into -ana.

DERIVATIVE VERBS.

Kupenda, *to love.*
Kupendana, *to love one another.*

Verbs ending in -e, -i, or -u make their reciprocal upon their applied forms.

Kuharibu, *to destroy.*
Kuharibiana, *to destroy one another.*

What are the reciprocal forms denoting—

To accuse one another. To answer one another. To annoy one another. To call one another. To cheat one another. To cure one another. To defend one another. To fear one another. To feed one another. To find one another. To forgive one another. To hate one another. To help one another. To take leave of one another. To meet with one another. To please one another. To praise one another. To scorn one another. To teach one another. To tell one another.

NEUTER VERBS.

A neuter verb, with a signification approaching that of the passive, is formed by changing the final -a into -ka.

Kufungua, *to unfasten,*
Kufunguka, *to be unfastened.*

Where the final -a is preceded by a consonant, or the verb ends in -e, -i, or -u, the neuter is made from the applied form.

Kuvunja, *to break.*
Kuvunjika, *to be broken.*
Kukata, *to cut.*

Kukatika, *to part, come in two.*
Kuharibu, *to destroy.*
Kuharibika, *to be destroyed.*

Verbs ending in -sha change -sha into -ka to form the neuter.

Kustusha, *to startle.*
Kustuka, *to be startled, to start.*

What are the neuter forms answering to—

To be wiped. To be washed. To be used. To be uncovered. To be torn. To be split. To be spilt. To be shaken. To be sewn. To be searched for. To be scorned. To be scattered. To be pulled. To be lifted up. To be lowered. To be passed. To be ground. To be forgotten. To be folded. To be bought. To be accepted. To be annoyed.

CAUSATIVE VERBS.

Verbs are made causative by changing their final syllable to -za or -sha.

Kupunguza, *to make less.*
Kutosha, *to make to give.*

Verbs ending in -ka change -ka into -sha.

Kushuka, *to go down.*
Kushusha, *to make to go down.*

Verbs ending in -ta change -ta into -sa.

Kufuata, *to follow.*
Kufuasa, *to make to follow.*

Verbs ending in -a preceded by a consonant,

DERIVATIVE VERBS.

and verbs ending in -e, -i, or -u, make their causatives on their applied forms.

> Kupenda, *to love*.
> Kupendeza, *to please*.
>
> Kuharibu, *to destroy*.
> Kuharibisha, *to make to destroy*.
>
> Kuzidi, *to become greater*.
> Kuzidisha, *to make greater*.

It is not easy to know when to use -za and when -sha. The first refers rather to causing an action, the other to causing a state. In the following lists the verbs in the first paragraph use -za, those in the second -sha. The third paragraph contains those which follow the previous rules.

What are the causative forms of—

1. Kuchukia. Kujaa. Kuzoea. Kufanya. Kuingia. Kugomba. Kukwea. Kushangaa. Kutulia. Kuchukua. Kugeua. Kuelea. Kuokoa. Kukataa. Kukimbia. Kulekea. Kutimia. Kupenya. Kuregea. Kukua. Kupoa. Kusikilia. Kupotea. Kujongea. Kusogea. Kulipa. Kutegemea. Kuenea. Kukwaa. Kulia.

2. Kuweza. Kujumla. Kubadili. Kukaribu. Kupanda. Kupofua. Kuvuma. Kukosa. Kusumbua. Kupatana. Kukoma. Kukutana. Kulingana. Kusulibi. Kufurahi. Kupigana. Kushiba. Kukopo. Kurudi. Kuinama. Kukwama. Kuziba. Kuthubutu. Kutatana, Kuwasili. Kustarehe. Kuthani. Kusafiri. Kutaajabu.

3. Kuepuka. Kuteta. Kutaabika. Kuondoka. Kuamka. Kupofuka. Kuchemka. Kutakata. Kuvuka. Kuokota. Kucheka. Kukauka. Kuanguka. Kukumbuka. Kuwaka. Kuruka. Kunyoka. Kutikita. Kufingirika. Kutota. Kukasirika. Kuzunguka.

Translate into Swahili.

Our work is done. We can now write Swahili like a man who was born in Zanzibar. The people will wonder at us. If a man asks us a question, we know words which are correct to answer him with.

SWAHILI EXERCISES.
KEY.

PLURAL OF SUBSTANTIVES.

(page 1)

Vitendo. Mishale. Vikapo. Mibuyu. Vitanda. Vibofu. Vipofu. Mifupa. Vitabu. Mipaka. Mizigo. Vifungo. Mizinga. Mitumbwi. Misafara. Mikufu. Viti. Wafalme. Watoto. Videvu. Minazi. Mibuni. Vitana. Wapishi. Vizibo. Vikombe. Mitende. Viziwi. Milango. Walevi. Wazungu. Vidole. Wavuvi. Viroboto. Mignu. Vivuko. Wageni. Michezo. Walinzi. Mikono. Vipini. Vitwa. Wachunga. Vilima. Viboko. Vibanda. Wakalimani. Visiwa. Visu. Vifuniko. Mistari. Midomo. Wajusi. Mikate. Vioo. Vitanzi. Wachiro. Milingote. Waganga. Misiba. Vinu. Milima. Vinwa. Walezi. Viapo. Wazee. Vitunguu. Wasimamizi. Michikichi. Vipande. Mito. Vipele. Miti. Wapagazi. Viazi. Vigai. Vifuko. Vitambaa. Vidaka. Vifaru. Mito. Watoro. Mitai. Watumishi. Vivuli. Viatu. Wagonjwa. Wajinga. Watumwa. Watwana. Vijakazi. Wajakazi. Wajoli. Mikeka. Vidonda. Mikuke. Mitambo. Mikia. Vijiko. Viko. Miji.

Mitego. Vilemba. Mizabibu. Visibau. Mitungi. Visima. Mijeledi. Wake. Wachawi. Vijana.

AGREEMENT OF ADJECTIVES.
(page 4)

Kitendo kibaya. Mshale mrefu. Vikapo vitupu. Mibuyu minene. Kitanda kipana. Mfupa mgumu. Kitabu kikukuu. Mizigo mizito. Kifungo kizuri. Mizinga mikubwa. Mtumbwi mfupi. Misafara migeni. Mkufu mnene. Kiti kipya. Wafalme wakuu. Mtoto mzuri. Videvu virefu. Mbuni mzuri. Vitana vidogo. Mpishi mvivu. Vizibo vigumu. Kikombe kitupu. Mitende mifupi. Milango mipana. Mlevi mkali. Wazungu wake. Kidole kinene. Wavuvi wawivu. Miguu mitupu. Kivuko kipana. Wageni wavivu. Mchezo mzuri. Walinzi wakali. Mkono mzima. Vipini virefu. Kitwa kikavu. Wachunga wabaya. Kilima kikubwa. Kibanda kikavu. Mkalimani mbaya. Visiwa vikubwa. Kisu kikali. Vifuniko vizito. Mstari mrefu. Midomo mikavu. Wajusi wakubwa. Mkate mtamu. Vioo vipya. Kitanzi kirefu. Wachiro wake. Mlingote mfupi. Mganga mgeni. Misiba mizito. Kinu kipya. Milima mikubwa. Vinwa vipana. Walezi wawivu. Kiapo kichungu. Wazee wazuri. Kitunguu kibovu. Wasimamizi wakali. Michikichi midogo. Vipande vifupi. Mto mgumu. Miti mirefu. Mpagazi mvivu. Viazi vibichi. Kigai kikali. Vifuko vitupu. Kitambaa kikukuu. Vidaka vipana. Wajinga wageni. Mtumwa mpya. Wajakazi wavivu. Watwana wabaya.

SWAHILI EXERCISES: KEY.   139

Mjoli mwivu. Vidonda viwazi. Mkuke mzito. Mito mipana. Kiatu kipya. Watumishi wabaya. Kivuli kirefu. Mikeka mikukuu. Kijiko kidogo. Mikia mirefu. Kiko kifupi. Miji mikubwa. Mtego mtupu. Vilemba vizuri. Mzabibu mzuri. Visibau virefu. Mtungi mtupu. Mijeledi mizito. Mke mwivu. Viazi vikubwa vibichi. Mizigo mingapi? Vibanda vingapi? Mikate mingapi? Wapishi wangapi? Milima mingapi? Wajinga wangapi? Miji mingapi? Vipande vingapi? Mitungi mingapi? Visu vingapi?

NUMBERS.

(page 7)

Mtu mmoja. Kilemba kimoja. Kisu kimoja. Mti mmoja. Kifuko kimoja. Mtumwa mmoja. Mto mmoja. Mtungi mmoja. Mizigo miwili. Vifungo vitatu. Mizinga minne. Mitumbwi mitano. Misafara sita. Mikufu saba. Viti vinane. Wafalme kenda. Watoto kumi. Mnazi mdogo mmoja. Mibuni mikubwa miwili. Vitana virefu vitatu. Wapishi wavivu wanne. Vizibo vibaya vitano. Vikombe vidogo sita. Mitende mikubwa saba. Milango mipana tissa. Wazungu wafupi kumi. Kidole kinene kimoja. Miguu mipana mitatu. Vipini virefu vinne. Vilima vikubwa vitano. Vibanda vipya saba. Wakalimani wabaya wanane. Visu vikali kenda. Mistari mirefu kumi. Mchiro mkali mmoja.

THIS AND THAT.

(page 9)

Kitendo kizuri hiki. Mishale mirefu ile. Mbuyu mnene huu. Vitanda vile. Kibofu hiki. Mifupa migumu hii. Kitabu kikubwa hiki. Mpaka huu. Mizigo mizito ile. Vifungo hivi. Mizinga mikubwa ile. Msafara huu. Mikufu hii. Kiti kile. Wafalme wale. Watoto hawa. Mnazi huu. Mbuni ule. Vitana hivi. Mpishi huyu. Kizibo hiki. Kikombe kile. Mtende ule. Milango hii. Mlevi huyu. Wazungu hawa. Kidole hiki. Wavuvi wale. Miguu ile. Mguu huu. Kivuko hiki. Mgeni huyu. Michezo hii. Walinzi hawa. Mikono hii. Vipini hivi. Mchunga yule. Kilima kidogo hiki. Vibanda vidogo vile. Wakalimani wale. Visiwa vikubwa vile. Kisu kirefu kile. Kifuniko hiki. Mistari minene hii. Midomo minene hii. Wajusi wazuri wale. Mikate mitamu ile. Mlingote mrefu ule. Mlima mkubwa ule. Wazee hawa. Vitunguu vibichi vile. Kipele hiki. Mti ule. Wapagazi wavivu wale. Viazi vidogo hivi. Kigai kikali kile. Vitambaa vikukuu vile. Mjinga yule. Watumwa wavivu hawa. Mkuke mzito mfupi ule. Kiatu kikukuu kile. Watumishi wale. Mikeka mipya ile. Kiko hiki. Mitego hii. Vilemba vizuri vile. Visibau vizuri hivi. Mitungi mipya hii. Kisima hiki. Wachawi hawa.

(page 10)

Watu hawa wakali. Milima hii mikubwa. Watumwa hawa wavivu. Miti ile midogo. Mtu yule mfupi. Mkuke huu mzito. Wazungu hawa wawivu.

PERSONAL PRONOUNS.

(page 10)

Mimi mkali. Wewe mfupi. Yeye mkubwa. Wao wadogo. Sisi wazito. Ninyi wakavu. Hivi (*or* vile) vipya. Hiki (*or* kile) kikukuu. Hivi (*or* vile) vikukuu. Huu (*or* ule) mnene. Wao wavivu. Hivi (*or* vile) vibivu. Yeye mdogo. Yeye mkali. Yeye mgeni. Mimi mwivu. Ninyi wawivu. Wao wazuri. Huu (*or* ule) mtupu. Yeye mfupi. Wewe mkubwa. Ninyi wakubwa.

(page 11)

Mti huu u mdogo. Mtende ule u mfupi. Mzee huyu yu mkuu. Tu wakavu. Miti ile i mirefu. Mtu mdogo yule yu mkali. Kisu kile ki kikali. U mvivu. Yu mvivu. Yu mdogo. Yu mzuri. Yu mfupi. Ki kizito. Ki kirefu. Ki kibichi. Vi vibivu. Wa wazuri. U mfupi. Ki kikukuu. Vi vikukuu. Vi vipya. Vi vipya. I mibovu. Ki kipya.

(page 12)

Mshale ule umevunjika. Kikapo kimeanguka. Mbuyu umeanguka. Kitanda kikukuu kile kimevunjika. Mzee amekufa. Mfupa mkubwa umevunjika. Kitabu kipya kimepasuka. Mpaka umeonekana. Mzigo mzito umeanguka. Vifungo vimevunjika. Mitumbwi imeonekana. Msafara mkubwa umeonekana. Mikufu minene imevunjika. Mkufu umeanguka. Wafalme wakuu wamekufa. Mtoto mdogo amekufa. Mnazi mrefu ule umeanguka. Mtungi mkukuu umevunjika. Kitana kidogo kimevunjika. Mpishi ameonekana. Kikombe kimevunjika. Vikombe vipya hivi vimevunjika. Mitende miwili imeanguka. Milango minne imevunjika. Mlevi yule ameanguka. Wazungu saba wamekufa. Vidole viwili vimevunjika.

INTERROGATIVES.

(*page* 14)

Watu gani hawa? Mishale ipi? Vikapo gani? Mbuyu upi? Kitanda gani hiki? Nani mzee huyu? Mfupa gani huu? Vitabu vipi? Vifungo gani? Mtumbwi upi? Mkufu gani? Kiti kipi? Wafalme gani hawa? Mtoto yupi? Minazi ipi? Mtende upi? Nani mlevi huyu? Mfalme gani mlevi huyu? Miti gani ile? Mkono upi? Mchezo gani huu? Kilima kipi? Visiwa vipi vile? Kitu gani kisu hiki? Mtu gani mkalimani huyu? Mlingote upi? Msiba gani? Milima gani ile? Mti gani mchikichi? Nini kiapo? Msimamizi gani kipofu? Mzee yupi kiziwi? Yupi mganga? Mti gani? Miti ipi?

THE VERBS.

(*page* 20)

Nimekubali. Utashtaki. Tumepatana. Vitabadili. Watasumbua. Nilijibu. Inazaa. Kipofu anaomba. Ninasadiki. Wafalme wamefika. Wajinga wanauliza. Kiboko anaamka. Tutaoga. Viroboto watauma. Watoto wanajisifu. Watoto wanne wamezaliwa. Wazungu wamenunua. Mpishi alijenga. Mlinunua. Wazee waliita. Anaangalia. Wapagazi wanachukua. Msimamizi alidaka. Mtende ume-geuka. Waganga wamedanganya. Mfalme atachagua. Wachunga wanapiga makofi. Mtoto atapanda. Mzungu atashinda. Ninafikiri. Mpishi amepika. Wanakohoa. Kifuniko kilifunika. Msafara ule umevuka. Watoto hawa watalia. Watumwa watalima. Visu vikali vile vitakata. Wajakazi wanacheza. Misiba inapungua. Watumwa wabaya wale wanakawia. Watwana walichimba. Tutagawanya. Amefanya. Watumwa wale wameteka maji. Nimepiga mstari. Mzee yule aliota. Kitunguu kimekauka. Walevi wanapigana. Mshale uliingia. Miti mirefu ilianguka. Wazungu sita wamelewa. Mkate umeoza. Wajakazi wanasaga. Mfalme alitangulia. Ulisikiliza. Utapika. Ninatafuta. Mzee ameoa. Kipande kile kimeyeyuka. Watalipa. Tuliokota. Mfalme mkali alifanikiwa. Unasukuma. Ninasoma. Mfalme alikataa. Mtumwa alijuta. Wapagazi wanapumzika. Mkono ule unavimba.

THE OBJECTIVE PREFIX.

(*page* 22)

Kitendo hiki kinanisumbua. Mshale ulimpiga. Mishale ile iliwakosa. Anachukua vikapo sita. Mibuyu mitatu imeanguka. Wameleta vitanda viwili. Wamevileta vitanda viwili. Utaiacha mifupa. Nimekiona kitabu. Wameipita mipaka. Wapagazi sita wanaichukua mizigo kenda. Unakifungua kifungo. Watu kumi wanaikokota mizinga mikubwa miwili. Watu sita waliusukuma mtumbwi. Ninaona msafara. Uliiona misafara miwili. Ataufunga mkufu. Mfalme ameleta kiti. Nitakipata kiti kile. Wafalme watanilipa. Nilikuta watoto wanne. Umewapita watoto. Wazungu wameikata minazi.

Mpishi ameuvunja mtungi huu. Kijakazi amepata kitana kizuri. Mchunga anampiga mpishi. Ninataka mpishi. Nimekikata kizibo. Ameokota kikombe. Mitende miwili ile inazaa. Mlango umeoza. Wazungu wamemua mpishi mvivu yule. Kidole hiki kinaniuma. Wavuvi kumi wanarudi. Nimeua viroboto saba. Kipini kiliupiga mguu. Waliwaona wageni. Walinzi walikimbia. Waliinua mikono miwili. Tuliiona mikono. Tulipita vilima viwili. Wazungu waliua viboko sita. Wageni walijenga vibanda viwili. Mfalme alivitoketeza vibanda viwili. Mkalimani mdogo alijisifu. Mkalimani alinionyesha visiwa vikubwa viwili. Umekipokea kisu. Mpishi anakisugua kifuniko. Alinionyesha mstari. Mgeni ameukata mkate. Nimevivunja vioo. Milingote miwili imevunjika. Nimeuona mlima mdogo. Mlezi anawalisha watoto. Wazee wanasikiliza. Nimevionja vitunguu. Msimamizi anawapiga watumwa. Ninatafuta mchikichi. Mchiro amekiuma kipande kile. Mtumwa ataleta mto. Miti imefika. Nitawalipa wapagazi. Viazi vimeoza. Wataviseta vigai. Alikileta kifuko kitupu. Tulikitatua kitambaa. Niliona vidaka sita. Watumwa walijipenda. Mfalme anajisifu. Umejifunga. Watoto walijilisha. Watajithuru. Wajinga wanajipindua. Watumwa wavivu wajikuna.

VOWEL ROOTS.

(*page* 25)

Niliona watu wekundu wanne. Watu weusi wawili waliona mtu mweupe. Mstari huu mwembamba. Nilipiga mstari mweusi. Moto unawaka. Mizigo hii mepesi. Mizigo meusi ile mizito. Moyo mwepesi. Moshi mzito. Tutauona moshi mweusi. Tutaacha mioto mikubwa miwili. Umeisahau mioyo ile. Miaka ile mifupi. Waalimu wawili walinifundisha. Mwamba mweupe umezama. Nimemwambia mwamuzi. Waamuzi wanne walitusikia. Utamwita mwandishi. Niliusikia mwanzo mbaya. Mianzo mema miwili. Waashi wawili walijenga vibanda viwili. Mwashi huyu alitumia miti mingi. Wazungu walinunua miavuli mikubwa mingi. Wanaikata miembe mema ile. Tumewapita wenyewe. Mwezi mzuri umezama. Miezi hii mema, ile mibaya. Miiba miwili iliuingia mkono. Miiko hii mikubwa mizuri. Wevi walikimbia. Wevi werevu wawili waliutwaa mtumbwi. Waoga walimwogopa mzee.

(page 27)

Chakula chema. Mvuvi amekitwaa chambo. Vyango vyeusi vitano hivi. Nimenunua vyanu vikubwa kumi. Cheo hiki kifupi. Nimepata vyeti viwili. Aliona chombo chekundu kimoja. Nimeona vyombo vyeusi sita. Vyura vyerevu kumi. Chuma kizito. Vyuma hivi vyepesi. Umeleta chungu chekundu kimoja. Nitataka vyungu vyeusi vidogo vitatu. Utakichukua chuo kikubwa kile. Anachukua vyuo vyekundu vinene viwili. Nilikitwaa chusa kikubwa.

VOWEL TENSES.

(page 28)

Mfalme ataka chombo kikubwa. Mwembe mkubwa walianguka. Kisu hiki chataka kipini kikubwa. Mfalme apenda wazee. Waashi wataka miavuli mekundu. Miti yakizunguka kibanda. Chambo champendeza. Watumwa walinichukia. Wageni walituogopa. Kifuniko chafunika vyungu viwili. Waliviona vyeti. Chakula hiki chapendeza. Vitabu vyalifika. Walizaliwa. Alijisifu. Waliamka. Miti mirefu yalianguka. Aliufunga mlango. Nampenda mzoe. Twawachukia. Waliwaona watumwa weusi wanne. Watumwa weusi wanne waliwaona. Kibanda chanipendeza.

THE POSSESSIVE CASE.

(*page* 29)

Nalikitwaa kisu cha Mzungu. Nitauona mji wa mfalme. Utakiuma kitwa cha mzee. Nimekiona kisibau cha mlevi. Tumekipita kisima cha Mzungu. Nauona moshi mweusi wa moto mkubwa. Wanaviteketeza vyuo vya kiziwi. Watumwa wa mfalme waliutwaa mtumbwi wa mvuvi. Kisu cha mtumwa chaliupiga mkono wa mgeni. Wameuficha mlingote wa mtumbwi. Kiapo cha mzee. Misiba ya mgeni. Mikufu ya mtumwa mvivu. Mizigo ya wapagazi. Mlango wa mpishi. Midomo ya mlezi. Mishale ya watoto. Kibanda cha kipofu. Mkia wa mchiro. Mchiro ameuuma mkono wa mtoto. Viatu vya Mzungu.

POSSESSIVE PRONOUNS.

(*page* 31)

Mfalme wetu ameua mtumwa wako. Wazungu wamekata mitende yao. Mnazi wangu unazaa. Kisu chake kikali. Mshale wake ulinipiga. Chombo kikubwa chao kimezama. Walipenda chakula chao. Kibanda chetu kimeanguka. Mitiyako yanipendeza. Mzee ataka kisibau changu. Kitwa changu kinaniuma. Mkono wangu unaugusa mti. Naona kipini chake. Nalichukua mkufu wake. Mikufu yako mizito. Utawatwaa watumwa wetu. Nitaiacha mishale yako. Vitendo vyao vimetupendeza. Mtamchukia mfalme wetu. Watu wetu wachukia wageni. Amekificha kisu changu. Mtu wangu anatwaa kisibau chako. Mikuke yao mirefu. Moyo wa mvuvi mwepesi. Moshi wa moto wao mwingi.

HIM AND HIS.

(page 31)

Nalimpiga mguu. Alinipiga kitwa. Nalimfunga miguu. Waliniuma mikono. Mchiro alimuma kidole. Watumwa walinikata kitwa. Kisu chalinigusa mkono. Wajakazi walimsugua miguu. Alinikuna mkono. Mfalme alimfungua mtumwa mikono. Amejiuma jicho. Atajifunga mikono.

ALL, HAVING, ITSELF, BY ITSELF.

(page 33)

Watumwa wote. Vitu vyote. Miti yote. Watumwa wote wenyi vibanda. Vitu vyote vyenyi mwisho. Miti yote peke yao. Nalimwona peke yake. Naliwaona watu hawa wote wawili. Naweza peke yangu kuuinua mtungi huu. Mlituona sote. Watakimbia wote. Wataitupa mikuke yote. Wevi walivitwaa vilemba vyetu vyote. Tumeviona vyote. Naliona vivuli vitatu, waliona kimoja peke yake. Naliona mibuyu miwili, uliiona yote. Nalimwona kiboka mwenyewe. Naliiona milima yenyewe. Wafalme wenyi vilemba waliniambia. Mchiro mwenyi mkia. Mti mwenyi miiba miingi. Naliwaambia wazee sita wenyi miavuli. Mfalme mwenyewe aliitwaa mikuke yote yenyi vipini vizuri. Nalisimama peke yangu. Twalitazama sote. Miiko yalikimbia peke yao. Mchawi aliiona yote. Mchawi aliwadanganya wevi wote wawili. Walitafuta wote. Mwezi mwote umeonekana. Vyombo vyote vitazama. Vitabu vikubwa vyote.

THE RELATIVE.

(page 36)

Muungu anayeniona. Ninyi mnaomwabudu Muungu. Watu walioabudu miungu mingi. Kivuli kinachopita. Wajakazi wanaochukua mitungi. Mtu atakayetupa mkuke. Mkuke utakaonipiga. Utakayeuona mkuke. Mkuke wake utakaoniua. Wanaomjua. Wataijua miti itakayoanguka. Miti itakayoanguka itakiseta kibanda chako. Mtumwa aliyeleta kiti. Kiti kilichovunjika. Aliyekivunja kiti. Wajoli wake watakaompiga. Wajakazi watakaocheka. Wajinga watakaokimbia. Mzungu atakayeuvuka mto. Mzungu atakayezama. Watumishi waliopenda viazi. Viazi vinavyooza. Mzabibu unaozaa. Naliuona mtende uliozaa. Utakiona kidonda kinachomuma. Wagonjwa watakaotaajabu. Mganga atakayewaponya. Wajinga watakaomlipa mchawi aliyewadanganya. Mfalme anayempenda mke wake. Mfalme aliyewapenda watoto wake. Mpishi aliyepika chakula changu.

Mtumishi aliyeleta chakula changu. Chakula chema kilichowaua wote.

(page 37)

. Kitendo ulichokifanya. Kitanda ulichokivunja. Mfupa aliouokota. Kitabu walichokitwaa. Mpaka utakaoupita. Mizigo waliyoichukua wapagazi. Mfalme wanayemua. Watoto aliowazaa. Mlango ninaoufunga. Wazungu utakaowaona. Kidole alichokiuma. Mgeni wanayempiga. Kilima ulichokiona. Kiboko waliyemua. Kibanda alichokijenga. Mzee waliyemsukuma. Vitunguu mlivyovipenda. Kipande mtakachokipokea. Mti utakaouweka.

(page 38)

Nitakapomwona. Mgeni alipoanguka. Mzungu anakorudi. Mtende utakapozaa. Tunaposimama. Watu weusi walikokimbia. Chumba alimokaa kitako. Wavuvi walipoupindua mtumbwi wetu. Mfalme alipopita. Mzee atakapoondoka. Aliyeniona nani? Nani anayetoka?

IMPERATIVE AND SUBJUNCTIVE.

(page 40)

Mwite mtu aliyekupiga, nimwone. Mpige aogope. Nimemwona mtu uliyemua, nimzike? Nitamshtaki nikusumbue. Mwambie anijibu. Nakuomba, unisadiki. Tumepatana tuoge sote. Vivunje vyungu vile. Tuvivunje visu hivi? Vivunjeni vyote. Watunze watoto hawa. Ichukueni mizigo hii. Chague mtu mmoja apande. Vipike viazi hivi. Vikusanye viazi vile nivipike. Mwambie akifunike chungu. Viharibuni vibanda vyote. Tumevigawanya vitu alivyotuamuru tuviharibu. Tufanye nini? Mtumwa aikokote miti mirefu. Wajakazi wateke maji. Mfukuza kipofu. Kiziwi akae. Akutaka umsayidie. Atarudi awaamue watu wabaya. Uokote mkuke alioutupa mfalme aliyelewa aniue. Nalijaribu kumpiga teke. Waliukaribia mti waupande. Nalifuata niwazuie. Alivua aoge. Watu walikimbia waokoke. Mfalme alipeleka watumwa wawili wanitafute. Naligeuka nikifunue chungu. Mwivi alifika aupate mwavuli, wakalimani wawili wangu wakarudi wamzuie. Sisi watatu tulishuka tukilinde kibanda.

THE KA- TENSES.

(page 42)

Katokeni. Kamwite. Kaununue. Kainunue. Kawafukuze. Akakitwae. Enenda kamsayidie. Nijibu kaangalie. Alitangulia akafika. Alipita akarudi. Aliniuliza nikamwambia. Alikuuliza ukamwambia. Sikieni kanijibuni. Mlitazama, mkaiona miti. Nalikitafuta kisu nikakiona. Watumwa waliuona mwavuli wako uliouacha wakauleta, nikawaambia, mwenyewe atarudi, wakaniambia huyu amjua. Wageni walifika wakauteketeza mji wetu. Mzungu aliudaka mkuke wangu, akauvunja, nikampiga, akawaambia watu waliomfuata, mueni yule, nikakimbia, nikaokoka. Alivaa viatu vipya vyake, vikamuma. Nalichoka, miguu yangu ikavimba. Mfalme aliwaita watu wake akawaambia, mzee huyu mchawi, mshikeni, kamfungeni, wakamfunga. Watu waliomlinda, wakalewa wakalala, nikamfungua akikimbia. Watu wakaamka, wakasema, mchawi ameokoka. Wakamtafuta. Wakanikuta, wakaniambia, wamkumbuka mtu tuliyemfunga. Nikawaambia, mtu yupi? Wakaniambia, mchawi yule, amekimbia, mfalme wetu atatupiga. Nikawaambia, nitawaonyesha mji wake; nifuateni mtamwona, nikatangulia, wakafuata wote. Tukakukuta, ukatuambia, rudini, mzee amewadanganya. Mtoto alianguka akalia. Alinionyesha kidonda chake nikakiponya. Naligeuka, nikatazama. Nalikitwaa kiazi, nikakionja. Walilewa wakagombana. Aliondoka, akaimba. Mlisikitika, nikafurahi. Alingoja nikapita.

THE -KI- TENSE.

(page 44).

Mti ukianguka. Mti ukianguka. Mti ukianguka. Mti ukianguka. Mti ukianguka. Nikitazama. Ukitazama utawaona watu weusi wakikimbia. Mfalme akifika tutamwambia. Kisu kikimkata kidole, mtoto atalia. Akikileta kitabu nitaweza kusoma. Akileta kitabu ninachokijua. Nikiknsikia ukinena nitakujibu. Nawasikia wakikuita. Mkifika mwulizeni. Mkirudi, angalieni. Ukinipiga angalia. Akikuua nitawaua watoto wake wote. Mke wake akiniua atamsamehe. Ukiwapenda watoto wako, uwapige. Ukinipenda uwasamehe. Kiziwi akikusikia mwambie. Ukimleta kipofu tutampiga. Watafuteni wevi, mkiwaona waleteni. Akiniuliza umjibu wewe. Nikimsikia akiita nitarudi. Nikimwona akitazama, nitauficha mtungi. Ukiuona mbuyu, umefika. Nawaona wapagazi wakikimbia, wanaacha mizigo yao, wageni wakiiona wanaitwaa. Tukikawia tutafanikiwa. Nikirudi rudini ninyi nyote. Tukirudi, turudi sote. Kibanda kinaanguka, tukitoka tutaokoka. Akipiga mbio nitampita. Kibanda kikiharibika, jenga chingine. Akifanya mtumbwi, uvunjeni. Akikumbuka tutamlipa. Akileta mkuke tutauvunja. Mpishi akipika chakula chema tutamsifu. Akiharibu chakula chema ɪ́fitampiga. Akiuvunja mtungi ataogopa. Akioga alizama. Mzungu alimwona akizama, akakimbia. Akiinua mkono, kisu chalianguka, kikianguka kikamkata.

CONDITIONAL TENSE.

(page 45)

Kama ningalimsikia, ningaliogopa. Kama kisu kingalianguka, kingalinikata. Kama ungalimwambia mfalme angaliwaua. Ungalikiteketeza kibanda chake. Mngaliviteketeza vibanda vyao. Kama mitumbwi yao ingalirudi, tungaliokoka. Mkuke ungalimpita. Mlevi angaliua mtoto wake. Kama angalitazama, mke wake angalimwona. Kama angaliangalia, mke wake angalirudi. Nalimwona akipita, ukaniambia, amefanya mtumbwi. Nikamwambia, huyu asema umefanya mtumbwi nataka kuutazama. Akaniambia, kama ungaliwauliza watumwa wangu, wangalikuonyesha mtumbwi wangu. Nikamwambia nionyeshe mwenyewe. Nikauona nikataajabu. Kama mngaliuona mngalitaajabu.

NEGATIVE PRESENT.

(page 47)

Mfalme wetu hapendi Wazungu. Wazungu hawapendi waganga wetu. Watumwa wavivu hawapendi msimamizi. Mto hauipiti mibuyu ile. Siwaoni watu wetu. Hamnipendi. Siwachukii. Hasomi. Mitumbwi haizami. Huangalii. Hawa wanaandika, wale hawaandiki. Nalimwambia, uliyemwona yupi? Akaniambia simwoni. Hawafundishi watoto wangu. Mzee haamki. Watoto wao hawalii. Minazi yao haizai. Mtende wangu unazaa, mitende yako haizai. Hakipendi chusa kile. Milingote ile inaanguka. Mtumbwi wake hauzami. Haharibu kibanda chako. Sisahau vitendo vyako. Hanisamehe. Hawatujibu. Humsadiki. Hafikiri. Hawakuamuru. Siwasifu. Sirudi. Hatutharau. Huthani. Hatusafiri. Sitaajabu. Hawamwabudu Muungu. Watumwa hawa si wavivu.

NEGATIVE PAST.

(*page* 48)

Sikukubali. Hatukupatana. Sikujibu. Wafalme hawakufika. Wazungu hawakununua. Mpishi hakujenga. Hamkununua. Waanawake wale hawakuteka maji. Wazungu sita hawakulewa. Mfalme hakutangulia. Mzee hakukataa. Mshale haukumpiga. Hawakuvileta vitanda viwili. Wazungu hawakuikata minazi. Wazungu hawakuua viboko sita. Mkalimani hakunionyesha visiwa. Wageni hawakujenga vibanda. Sikuvionja vitunguu. Hatukukitatua kitambaa. Sikumwambia mzee. Mwashi huyu hakutumia miti miingi. Waoga hawakumwogopa mjakazi. Waashi hawakutaka miavuli miekundu. Mtumwa hakumchukia. Vitabu havikufika. Hakujisifu. Hawakuwaona watumwa weusi wanne.

(*page* 50)

Mgeni hajaukata mkate. Mlezi hajawalisha watoto. Hawajavileta vitanda viwili. Sijakiona chuo. Hajaufunga mkufu bado. Wafalme hawajanilipa bado. Hawajawapita watoto. Mtende haujazaa. Wazungu hawajaikata minazi. Mpishi mvivu hajakisugua kifuniko. Wavuvi hawajauleta mtumbwi bado.

NEGATIVE FUTURE AND CONDITIONAL.

(*page* 51)

Hatarudi. Hatutamwona. Hatungalimwona. Kama hungalifika, hangalituona. Mfalme wetu hatawapenda Wazungu wale. Wazungu hawangalipenda waganga wetu. Watumwa wavivu hawangalipenda msimamizi mkali. Hamtawaona watu wetu. Wazungu hawangalilala. Watu weusi hawangalikimbia. Mitumbwi haingalivunjika. Minazi hii haingalizaa. Hawangalikuamuru. Hatanisamehe. Hatutasafiri. Mzee hatarudi. Wajinga wale hawatatujibu. Singalimpenda. Singalikwambia.

NEGATIVE SUBJUNCTIVE.

(*page* 52)

Tusione. Asirudi. Mfalme asitwambie. Usitazame. Msitazame. Usimwambie. Mpige asifanye. Usinene, wasisikie. Waambie wasikitafute. Tusiupite. Mshike mtoto asianguke. Vifiche vitabu wasisome. Waambie wasisikilize. Nitarudi nisiwakute. Msivute. Waambie wapagazi wasiichukue mizigo miwili hii.

SWAHILI EXERCISES: KEY. 155

Usitwae mkuke wangu. Usiteketeze kibanda changu. Msimfanye mfalme. Usilewe. Angalie kisu kisikukate kidole. Angalie usimpige Mzungu yule. Usiwasifu vijakazi. Usikilete kitabu, sijui kusoma. Usinene nisikujibu. Ukimua, usiwaue watoto wake.

NEGATIVE WITH RELATIVES.

(page 53)

Kivuli kisichopita. Wajakazi wasiochukua mitungi. Mtu asiyetupa mkuke. Naliona watu watatu usiowaona. Usiyeuona mkuke utakipita kibanda. Wasiomjua. Nisiyemjua. Miti isiyoanguka haikuseta kibanda chako. Kiti kisichovunjika. Wajinga wasiokimbia. Mzungu asiyeuvuka mto. Wazungu wasiouvuka mto. Watumishi wasiopenda viazi. Mti usiozaa. Wagonjwa wasiotaajabu. Mganga asiyewaponya wote. Wajinga wasiomlipa mchawi asiyewadanganya. Mfalme asiyempenda mke wake. Mfalme asiyewapenda watoto wake. Mpishi asiyepika chakula changu. Chakula chema kisichotuua.

NEGATIVE PARTICIPIAL TENSE.

(page 54)

Asipokupenda sitampenda. Wasipotoka wafalme hawataingia. Asipokaribu mwenyewe mleteni. Nisipongoja sitapata kisu chake. Mfupa usipovunjika, mkono utapona. Mzungu asipomua mpishi, hatawapendeza watu weusi. Usipompiga mtoto wako, atakutharau.

THE PASSIVE VOICE.

(page 56)

Nalipigwa, hukupigwa. Atapigwa na mtumwa. Wapigwe. Nisipigwe. Mzee ataumwa. Mkuke uliletwa. Vibanda viwili vinajengwa. Mfalme hajazikwa. Vijakazi wanaitwa. Mtumbwi utunzwe. Wazungu hawatashindwa. Chakula kimepikwa. Mji umeingiwa na wageni wanne. Mlango ungalifungwa. Siogopwi. Watoto hawajalishwa bado. Sikuificha mikuke, imefichwa na wenyewe. Kama ningalimwambia singalipendwa na Wazungu. Kipande kimewekwa wapi? Mchawi hapendezwi. Hutakumbukwa. Mfalme wako hatakumbukwa na watoto wetu. Kioo hakijarudishwa. Kibanda kifagiwe na mjakazi. Watoto wasifundishwe na Mzungu. Naliambiwa na mtumwa wake. Mkuke ulitupwa na mwivi.

ADVERBS.

(page 59)

Nimenunua mkuke mzuri sana. Haoni vema. Siwapendi sana watumwa wavivu. Nalimwona akirudi upesi. Singalijenga kibanda kikubwa sana. Nalitazama nyuma nikaona wageni wawili. Nalisikia mtu karibu, akiimba sana, nikathani huyu Mzungu nitakimbia upesi. Mfalme juu, watumwa chini. Niliona mtu akitazama, nikakwambia, anatuona sasa, ukaniambia, anatazama nje, sisi ndani, tupite polepole asitusikie, yamkini tutaokoka, tukapita, halafu akatoka mtu mwingine, nikasema, kweli hatuwezi kuokoka, ukasema, mtumwa tu, hawezi kutuzuia, tukampita. Nimewakumbuka marra nyingi watu wawili wale, wangalituua marra wote kama wangalitujua. Watoto walitangulia mbele, waana waume wakawafuata watoto, mwisho wakafuata wazee.

PREPOSITIONS.
(page 61)

Kilifanywa cha miti. Naona mtu akisimama juu ya mtumbwi. Akakipokea kwa mikono miwili. Naliununua mkuke kwa kitambaa kikukuu. Atarudi katika mji. Nalimkuta katika mji. Rudini kwa mfalme wenu. Alikaa katika mti. Akashuka katika mti, akapita hatta akawakuta wajoli wawili wake juu ya mti mwingine. Wakafika chini ya kilima. Watumwa wote walifuata nyuma ya mfalme. Akatangulia na watumwa wake katika kisiwa. Nalirudi kwa wenzi wangu tukamwona mwenyewe katika mtumbwi wake, tukamwambia, shuka katika mtumbwi wako, akajibu, vema, tukamfuate upesi mfalme wetu, tutamwona katika mji. Nikamwambia, hajafika katika mji wake, akatuambia, anafika sasa.

CONJUNCTIONS.
(page 63)

Kijana na mzee walinifuata katika mji. Mzee akasimama katika mlango na mkuke, nikamwambia. Umefika lini? Umeupata wapi mkuke ule? Wala hakunijibu, nikamwuliza tena. Marra nikamwona kijana tena, nami, nikamwuliza, mzee huyu ameupata wapi mkuke ule? Akaniambia mwulize mwenyewe. · Nikamwambia, nimemwuliza, lakini hanijibu. Akaniambia, labuda hakukusikia, sema sana. Nikasema sana, mzee akasema, mimi kiziwi, nakusikia ukisema tu, nisamehe. Nikamwambia, nawe nisamehe sikujua. Nikamwuliza tena nikisema sana, akaniambia, naliununua. Nikamwambia, lini? Kijana akaniambia, ao aliuiba ao aliuokota katika milima. Mzee akamwambia, wasema nini? Kijana akasema, alikusikia, naye kama kweli angaliununua angalikujibu marra. Nikamwambia, huyu mzee yamkini amesahau. Akaniambia, hasahau, lakini watu wa mji huu twamjua sana mwivi huyu tangu mtoto. Nikamwambia, ameiba nini? Akaniambia, vitu vingi, huyu mgeni alifukuzwa na mfalme wake katika mji wake hatta sasa anakaa katika mji wetu, wala hatumpendi lakini hatumfukuzi kwa sababu mchawi, nao watu wamwogopa. Nikataajabu nikimsikia, nikasema, sisadiki kama huyu mchawi ninyi nyote waoga, nanyi mnaogopa kivuli. Akaniambia, simwogopi kwani nathani waganga wetu waweza kumshinda. Nikamwambia mzee, umetusikia? Akaniambia, mimi kiziwi nawasikia mkisema tu, lakini usimsadiki akikwambia nimefukuzwa na mfalme wetu katika mji wangu. Sikufukuzwa, nami nitarudi. Kama ningalifukuzwa watu wa mji huu hawangalinikubali nikae katika mji wao. Nikamwambia, ao wewe si kiziwi, ao yakini amesema kweli wewe mchawi. Akaniambia mzee, sisikii. Nikageuka nikatoka katika mji wala sikumwambia mtu illa wewe, lakini namsadiki mzee wala kiziwi, wala mchawi, illa mtu mwerevu aliyeuiba mkuke, akataka kunidanganya, lakini nami najua kuwadanganya watu.

PLACE.

(page 66)

Nalipaona mahali waliposimama wavuvi, mtumbwi mpya wao ukizama. Nalipapita mahali penyewe. Naliona mahali penyi vibanda vyingi. Sulemani alifika mahali pako, nikamwuliza, umemwacha Abdallah wapi? niambie mahali, akaniambia mahali katika mji walipokaa wazee wake zamani. Nikamwambia sipajui. Akaniambia, ulipomwona ukiuvuka mto. Nikapukumbuka mahali, pazuri, karibu ya mto. Nikamwambia, napakumbuka sasa, tulipaona sote, mahali pazuri. Akaniambia, pazuri.

INFINITIVES OF VERBS.

(page 67)

Kukubali. Kushtaki. Kupatana. Kubadili. Sipendi kukupiga. Kujibu marra nyingi. Kuzaa kwingi. Kuona na kusadiki. Kujisifu si kwema. Kuchemka upesi. Kuleta si kutwaa. Kupika kwake kuzuri. Kulia kutakuthuru. Kwa kulima. Katika kucheza. Kwa kuchimba sana. Kwa kuota kuzuri na kufanya kubaya. Mtumwa mvivu anisumbua sana kwa kukawia kwake. Waliileta miti kwa kukokota. Aliokoka kwa sababu ya kuogopa. Naliwaona katika kupigana. Kusamehe na kusahau.

ADJECTIVES [MA- CLASS].

(page 71)

Jambo baya. Mapenzi makubwa. Malozi mabivu. Jibu kali. Tao pana. Majifu makavu.

Shoka zito. Maganda manene. Pipa dogo. Bakuli zima. Matuta marefu. Malengelenge makubwa. Majipu mapya. Machupa matupu. Kasha zito. Dafu tamu. Tone kubwa. Masikio marefu. Mayayi mabovu. Makosa mapya. Mainzi makali. Matunda matamu. Kaburi tupu. Tunda dogo. Maneno mazuri. Jani refu. Majani mafupi. Jamvi pana. Maziwa mabichi. Jina zuri. Shingo refu. Makasia mazito. Machungwa matamu. Manukato mazuri. Shamba kubwa. Mashairi mazuri.

Gote jororo. Tundu jembamba. Kaburi jingine. Makaburi mengi. Maji mengi. Tunda jekundu. Matunda mekundu marefu. Mainzi membamba. Makosa mengine. Macho meusi. Macho meupe. Jicho jekundu. Yayi jeupe. Mavumbi mepesi. Mashaka mengi. Dau dogo jembamba. Matumaini mema. Machupa mekundu mema. Bakuli jepesi. Shoka jema. Mashoka mepesi mema. Majibu merevu. Malozi mema. Mambo mepesi.

DEMONSTRATIVES [MA- CLASS].

(page 72)

Kasha kubwa hili. Masufuria makubwa yale. Matango haya. Masikio marefu yale. Kosa dogo hili. Tundu lile. Magote haya. Matone mepesi haya. Mashaka machungu yale. Jicho kupwa hili. Meno makubwa haya. Yayi bichi kubwa hili. Yayi bichi lile. Machupa yale. Maagizo haya. Majipu haya. Mapipa makubwa manne yale. Majifu makavu haya. Matao matano haya. Jibu lile. Malozi meupe haya. Shauri jema hili. Mambo mapya haya. Maji matamu yale. Mashoka makali haya. Shoka kali lile. Pipa lile. Pipa hili.

WHICH? [MA- CLASS].
(page 73)

Machupa yapi? Kasha lipi? Sikio lipi? Mayayi yapi? Jicho lipi? Matunda yapi? Tundu lipi? Shimo lipo? Gote lipi? Mapipa yapi? Shoka lipi? Makasia yapi? Fungu lipi? Maji yapi? Mafuta yapi? Tao lipi? Jino lipi?

PERSONAL PRONOUNS [MA- CLASS].
(page 74)

Nimelikubali shauri. Mambo haya hayapatani. Hutayabadili maagano. Majifu yanisumbua. Makanda yamefika. Maji yanachemka. Amelivunja bakuli. Leteni mapipa sita. Aliyelijenga kaburi nani? Tulivunje shoka. Nunua mayayi kumi. Usiyavunje mayayi. Walitunze tawa. Waanawake watachukua maji katika mitungi. Napenda kulitafuna ganda tamu hili. Hawakulisafisha jamvi. Twaliyakusanya machungwa. Mpishi wetu atayapika mananasi. Lifunike sufuria. Wameyaseta malozi. Tulikate lengelenge? Maziwa yanapungua. Watumwa walijaribu kulilinda zizi. Tuyagawanye mapapayi ao makorosho? Waliyamwaga mafuta. Mfalme hakuliingia shimo. Utayaona maboga mawili katika mlango. Walisahau kuyaleta makasia wakaleta makafi mawili tu. Kama wangalilitweka tanga, wangaliokoka. Kama hawangalilitweka tanga kubwa hawangalizama. Tunayatafuta matikiti, umeyaona?

POSSESSIVE PRONOUNS AND CASE [MA- CLASS].

(page 75)

Nalitwaa shoka la Mzungu. Nitaliona shamba la mfalme. Utamuma mzee jicho. Nimeliona kafi la mlevi. Tumelipita kaburi la Mzungu. Naona majifu meupe ya moto mkubwa. Wanayateketeza mananasi ya kiziwi. Watumwa wa mfalme walitwaa makafi ya mvuvi. Gote la mtumwa lilimpiga mgeni jicho. Wamelificha tanga la mtumbwi. Shingo la mzee. Majuto ya mgeni. Tumbo la mtumwa mvivu. Maagano ya wapagazi. Sufuria la mpishi. Mapenzi ya mlezi. Meno ya watoto. Mashauri ya kipofu. Sikio la mchiro. Mchiro amemuma mtoto kwapa. Jibu la Mzungu.

Mfalme wetu ameharibu shamba lako. Wazungu wamekata makuti yao. Tunda langu bivu. Shoka lake kali. Mshale wake ulinipiga shingo. Walipenda machungwa yao. Tao letu limeanguka. Vijakazi vyako vyalitwaa tawa langu. Mamumunye yako yanipendeza. Mzee ataka talasimu langu. Jino langu linaniuma. Shoka langu linaugusa mti. Naona tundu lake. Nalichukua machungwa yake. Jipu lako kubwa. Utatwaa manukato yetu. Nitaacha gari lako. Mazumgumzo yao yamenipendeza. Mtachukia mainzi yetu. Watu wetu wapenda mapapayi. Ameficha maziwa yangu. Mashairi yako mengi. Maziwa yetu, maji yenu na mafuta yao. Machukio yangu, mapenzi yako na majuto yao. Maagano yetu hayajaisha. Lengelenge langu si jipu lako.

Mambo yote. Mazumgumzo yote. Jibu lenyewe. Mapipa yenyewe. Mapipa yenyi maji.

Pipa lenyi mafuta. Tuta lenyi viazi. Majipu yote yaniuma. Lete mabakuli yote. Sikio lenyewe. Vunje majani yote kalete matunda yote. Maneno yenyi makosa.

THE RELATIVE [MA CLASS].
(page 77)

Machukio ninayoyaona. Mashauri niliyoyapokea. Mambo yaliyonisumbua. Maagano tuliyoyafanya, wewe na mimi. Malozi yaliyookotwa. Jibu atakalolitia. Tao linaloanguka. Majifu anayoyatawanya. Shoka litakaloukata mti ule. Mapipa waliyoyachukua watu wa mfalme. Bakuli nililolivunja. Lengelenge lillioniuma. Jipu lililoonekana. Gari wanalolivuta. Kanisa tunalolijenga katika mji. Matumaini watakayoyaona watumwa. Mainzi yanayonisumbua. Mafuta unayoyamimina. Shimo ulilolichimba. Manukato uliyoyanunua. Mananasi yanayopikwa. Matikiti wanayoyatafuta watoto. Tanga walilolitweka.

NEGATIVE TENSES [MA CLASS].
(page 78)

Mfalme wetu hayapendi malozi haya. Mambo haya hayanisumbui. Shoka hili halikati. Mazumgumzo haya hayanipendezi. Jibu lake halitoshi. Pipa halizami. Jicho halisikii. Sikio halioni. Maboga hayaruki. Mamumunye hayalii.

Bakuli halikufika. Shoka halikuniuma. Talasimu halikumthuru. Matalasimu yao hayakuwalinda. Ganda chungu halikukuponya.

Jambo halijaisha. Ganda chungu halijakuponya bado. Tone halijaanguka. Mayayi hayajapikwa. Maji hayajachemka bado. Jani halijakauka. Jibu kali halitamfukuza. Mananasi hayataoza. Mashairi haya hayatampendeza sana. Mashairi yako hayatampendeza mfalme. Maneno magumu hayatatuua. Majuto hayatanilipa. Matanga hayataugusa mlingote. Mayayi yasioze. Machungwa yasianguke. Maboga yasipikwe. Matunda yasisetwe. Majifu yasitunzwe. Mayayi yasianguke.

THE N CLASS, ADJECTIVES.
(page 86)

Hasara kubwa nyingi. Embe mbivu mbili. Alama nyeusi. Fetha nyeupe. Imbu moja. Sindano kali. Habari njema. Pua ndefu. Barua nane. Lulu nzuri. Kalamu njema. Nguzo nene. Ncha kali. Thamani kubwa. Robo tatu. Haja mpya. Dari njema. Nafasi nyingi. Nafasi nyingi. Kutu nyekundu. Parafujo ndefu. Akili chache. Dalili wazi. Ngozi kubwa. Sabuni nyororo. Nyota ndogo. Hali mbaya. Fimbo ndefu. Meza pana. Hema nyeupe. Hila nyerevu. Njia fupi. Ngano mbivu. Dawati nzuri. Nanga nzito. Pembe tatu. Nyama mbichi. Nguvu nyingi. Ndizi tamu. Ndevu ndefu. Damu nyeusi. Ndoo ndogo. Zulia kubwa. Sifa njema. Rungu nzito. Rangi nyeupe. Thiraa sita. Siku kumi. Sitaha nyembamba. Ndoto nyingi. Bandera mpya. Bustani nzuri.

PRONOUNS [N CLASS].

(*page* 88)

Hesabu zanisumbua. Fayida yanipendeza. Walizipokea sadaka. Nanga i nzito. Aliipiga pembe. Nyama zimekimbia. Anazitafuta nyama. Siafu zimetuuma. Mchwa zimeziharibu daftari. Boriti zi ndefu. Nimeisikia kengele. Watu wanne wanaichukua jeneza. Damu itanikumbusha. Naliziona ndoo tupu mbili. Naliivaa kofia, ikaniuma. Saa ikapiga. Nguo zataka kufungwa. Nalizinunua garofuu. Ndoto ikaisha. Njaa inaniuma. Wataitweka bandera. Bandera imetwekwa. Sikupata fayida. Nimeipata hasara. Twaisikia sauti.

DEMONSTRATIVES [N CLASS].

(*page* 89)

Nyumba hii kubwa. Bustani hii ndogo. Ajabu kubwa hii. Kabari nzito mbili hizi. Siki kali hii. Ishara ile. Ishara zipi? Ngozi kavu zile. Lulu nzuri zile. Embe tamu hizi. Fetha mpya hii. Sindano zipi? Haja hii. Taa hizi. Taa zipi? Hizi. Baruti hii. Hema zile. Inchi hii. Ndoo ipi? Zulia hii. Kofia zile. Nyumba zile. Saa hii. Nguo hizi.

POSSESSIVES [N CLASS].

(*page* 90)

Nimeona hesabu zake. Nionyeshe daftari yako. Fayida za Abdallah zapita zangu. Nimenunua ndizi zake zote. Boriti za nyumba yangu. Alimkata mzee ndevu. Watoto wanazipiga kengele mbili zetu. Alishusha ndoo yetu katika kisima chako. Mkuke wa Abdallah uliipiga ngao ya Ali. Shughuli zetu nyingi. Mabruki amevaa kofia nyekundu yangu. Saa yangu njema, yake mbaya. Nguo yake imetatuka. Tende zile zangu. Ndoto njema zetu. Tupa zenu. Taa zenu zinawaka. Sikukubali thahabu yake. Sijaona njugu zako. Hatuabudu sanamu zao. Waliona hema zenu. Sisikii sauti zao. Hawatapata haja yao. Hataniambia siri zake. Fanya kazi yako. Mganga hajui kuwaponya jeraha.

Nachukia zawadi zote. Zawadi zote zampendeza mfalme wetu. Bustani yenyi miti. Hema zenyi bandera. Ndizi zote zimeoza. Siagi yote imeyeyuka.

THE RELATIVE [N CLASS].
(page 91).

Jeraha niliyoiponya. Jeraha nisizoziponya. Nyota iliyofuata. Uliiona kazi waliyoifanya. Ngano itakayosagwa. Kabari mtu wetu aliyoitia chini ya mlango ililegezwa. Siki isiyooza ilimwagwa. Handaki aliyoichimba katika shamba lake ilifika hatta nyumba uliyoinunua. Naliziona dalili nilizoambiwa niziangalie. Haya yake imemwacha. Zitafute parafujo tulizoziona jana. Kutu inayoonekana leo, ilionekana jana. Haja zote atakazonyima mfalme leo nitazisikia halafu. Nafasi niliyoitaka ingalikutosha. Mvua iliyopita juu ya dari yetu iliingia katika nyumba mpya wanayoijenga. Ahadi niliyoitoa. Mfalme aliijua hila iliyowadanganya wageni. Fetha aliyoipokea mvuvi nyingi. Nitatoa robo ya thamani anayoitaka mwashi. Nguzo zilizosetwa zote kubwa. Lulu aliyoileta mvuvi hatukuiona kabisa.

NEGATIVE TENSES [N CLASS].
(*page* 92)

Fetha yote haingalitumiwa. Hesabu zake hazikunipendeza. Fayida hii haitakutosha. Hewa hii haitakuponya. Sadaka zao hazingalimpendeza Muungu. Hasira ya mfalme hainithuru. Sauti ya kengele haikunisumbua. Boriti hazikuoza. Galawa haijazama. Saa haipigi. Saa hazijapiga. Barua haifiki. Barua zenu hazikufika. Parafujo haiingii. Pua haoni.

ADJECTIVES [U CLASS].
(*page* 96)

Uzee mwingi. Ndevu ndefu. Udevu mrefu. Uzuri mwingi. Upindi mrefu. Pindi ndefu. Fagio ndogo. Kucha fupi. Ukucha mrefu. Ua mpana. Umande mwingi. Uso mzuri. Nyuso nzuri. Ukuni mdogo. Kuni kavu. Unga mweupe. Unga mwororo. Nyayo nyingi. Nyele nyekundu. Unyele mweupe. Unyele mnene. Wino mweusi. Funguo ndogo. Utambi mnene. Mbau nene. Ubau mwepesi. Pondo nzito. Mbau nyekundu mbili. Nataka pondo ndefu mbili. Nimenunua mbau njema tano. Nalisikia nyimbo tatu. Naliona unga mwingi. Nalikaa usiku mmoja.

PRONOUNS [U CLASS].
(page 98)

Upindi umevunjika. Uma wauma. Ufalme umefanikiwa. Naliumwaga wino. Umeme ulipiga mti ukaua watu watatu. Ukarasa uliletwa, ukatatuka. Ubau haukutakwa wenyi urefu mwingi. Mtoto alikata kuni akajiuma uso. Waliziona tambi nazo fupi sana. Ufalme ulishindwa. Nyayo hazionekani. Ukali wa mfalme wawasumbua watu wake. Mtoto alizitwaa funguo akazisugua. Ubishi uliwapendeza. Ukufi wa unga utatosha. Ulimwengu u mbaya. Urithi huu si mkubwa. Nalishika upanga wako. Aliokota wembe wangu akauleta. Ua ulifagiwa. Ufagio ulipotea. Nyavu zilivunjika zikaokoka nyama. Uvivu wa mtoto wanitoshea. Wembe huu mkali. Ubau huu mfupi. Ufalme mkubwa huu. Nyimbo hizi. Wali ule. Fagio zile. Pindi zipi? Ua mpana ule. Funguo zile zilipotea. Wamezivunja pondo zile zote. Uso mzuri ule. Unga mbaya huu. Uayo huu. Upanga mkali ule.

Upuuzi unaousema. Panga zile nilizozinunua. Alizinunua nyuma zile nilizozikataa. Zilianguka kuta nilizozijenga. Usiku wote watu walicheza wakafanya sauti nyingi. Nimeziokota funguo alizozisugua mtoto. Aliomba ukufi wa tende nikakataa. Sikupenda unyonge wake walipomtaka kutoa wali alioupika. Hawangaliuleta unga nilioutaka.

THE -NI CASE.
(page 99)

Mtu aliingia mtoni. Wakafuata nyumbani mwake. Waliona miti mingi bustanini. Alinisukuma hatta tukafika nyumbani kwetu. Waujua mtende mlangoni pangu? Alilala na chuo chake kwapani. Sijarudi mjini kwangu. Nitangoja chini ya mti njiani. Alitoka kisimani akafika mjini. Alishika upindi wake na mishale yake mkononi. Wakakimbia wakajificha nyumbani mwao. Walipofika mtoni watu njiani wakacheka, punda akaogopa, akapiga teke, akaanguka mtoni, akazama, mtu na kijana wakarudi nyumbani kwao.

INDECLINABLE ADJECTIVES.
(page 102)

Wewe thaifu. Nyumba yake safi. Mayayi yale rahisi. Watumwa wake amini. Killa mtu alichukua upanga. Vitabu ghali. Mti uliounnunua laini. Watoto hawa rathi na chakula chema chao. Watu wale si watumwa, wale huru. Makasha wanayoyafanya tayari. Pondo zao kamili. Misiba yako hafifu. Kazi yangu thaifu. Kazi yako bora. Walipeleka chokaa haba. Kanisa wanalolijenga imara. Kuua si halali. Mtu hodari yule anayepigana atamshinda thaifu. Ndizi bustanini mwao marithawa. Chakula wanachokikataa yabis. Watu wale wote masikini. Nalimwona utupu.

COMPOUND ADJECTIVES.

(*page* 104)

Vitabu hivi vya kale. Hajui dasturi za kiungwana. Baada ya wakati wa mvua pepo za baridi zaanza. Watu wa hila wadanganywa marra nyingi. Kazi haba yafanywa siku za giza. Mambo mabaya sana si ya milele. Nguo ya Kizungu i ghali. Waliteketeza mji wa kwanza walioushinda. Mtu wa heri amenunua nyumba ya kupendeza. Alimwaga kahawa ya moto. Mtu wa haki apendwa na mtumwa wake. Dasturi yetu kupita upande wa kushoto wa njia. Mtu wa akili alikataa kukaa katika nyumba ya pili. Walipika ugali wake katika chungu cha mwenyewe. Usivae nguo za watu. Ukuta wa mkono wa kuume wa nyumba ulianguka. Alijenga mwenyewe kibanda cha mviringo. Sultani anayafikiri mambo ya siri ya ufalme wake. Mfalme wa kishenzi alikiharibu kitabu cha thamani. Mwite mtu wa pili. Kata killa mti wa nne. Nyumba ya kenda ilianguka. Nitakulipa killa siku ya kumi.

ADJECTIVAL VERBS.

(*page* 108)

Sauti ya mtu imesikiliana. Watoto walipofuka. Mayayi yaliyotokoseka. Mitungi iliyovunjika. Funguo za watoto zimekatuka. Mwezi umeng'ara. Mguu wa mtoto umechubuka. Gote limefaganzi. Mlango umenakishiwa. Chakula kilirahisika. Mliko haitatakasika. Mbingu zimetakata. Maneno yako yameelea. Roho yako imefarajika. Umete-

SWAHILI EXERCISES: KEY. 171

ngenea sana. Upindi umepindana. Ametumaini. Umefathaika. Kamba imepotoka. Mtoto amepona. Chumba kimechafuka. Njia imekauka. Chakula kimetosha. Watumwa walichoka. Kazi yetu imesitawi. Msimamizi amelevuka. Miti imevia. Uzi umetatana. Kisibau chake kimekazana. Abdallah amesumbuka. Kanda limefumuka. Amefaa. Maagano yametanguka. Kijana amethoofika. Majaliwa amechoka na kazi. Mzee amekunjana. Uso uliokunjana. Lulu imenifaa. Mti uliovia. Sisikitiki kabisa. Kijakazi aliyenyamaza. Mtoto aliyeungua aogopa moto. Ulimwengu umeviringana. Kasha lililoviringa. Njia iliyoparuza. Kijana aliyetulia. Nyama iliyooza. Mwamba uliochongoka. Msimamizi aliyependeza. Hesabu imekamilika. Mzee aliyepooza. Dau limeelekea kwetu. Ua limefunuka. Njaa yangu imezidi. Mkate uliofanya ukungu. Njaa yangu imepunguka. Watumwa waliolewa. Wazungu walionenyekea. Mzigo umemlemea mpagazi. Ndizi zimekomaa. Mgeni anapumbazika.

RELATIVE WITHOUT NOTE OF TIME.
(*page* 109)

Mtu umpendaye amerudi. Mfalme umogopaye amepona. Jambo likuzuialo lanisayidia mimi. Moto uwakao nyumbani mwangu utapika nyama niletayo. Utapata chakula chote nikipikacho katika sufuria lako. Vitabu uvisomavyo havitakufaa. Utaona fayida uitafutayo. Mlango niufunguao sitaufunga.

NAMES OF ANIMALS.

(*page* 112)

Naliwaambia asikari wakamwita jemadari. Habeshia mrefu alimwambia wakili mkali. Tembo mkubwa aliumwa na siafu. Mchwa adui wetu. Nyani wakubwa wakaa mitini. Punda mweupe wa kinyozi alimpiga teke shangazi wangu. Nyuki wafanya asali. Vijana waliona ngamia, ndugu wao aliona ndege wazuri wawili. Sermala aliumwa na taandu. Nalimwona jumbe alinunua ng'ombe wengi, na jogoo, na kuku wengi, na mabata wakubwa. Naliona mbwa, aliumwa na mainzi. Marafiki wangu hawapendi mende. Kijakazi amenunua paa mzuri. Baba wangu alinunua matunda mengi, kibeti adui wake akayatwaa. Bibi aliogopa vyura wakubwa; bwana akasema, simba mkubwa na chui mkali waogopwa, lakini watu wa akili hawaogopi chura. Jini alifanya uchawi juu ya liwali, mama wake alitaka kuua nguruwe mkubwa na njiwa watatu; kasisi akamwambia, haya upuuzi. Baharia akioga, naliona papa, alikuja akamshika kwa meno yake. Nalinunua kondoo walionona wanane. Nyoka mwerevu alimtwaa ghafula sungura. Dobi alinunua punda, asikari wakampata, hatta wakimchukua, nge alimuma mguu. Kathi mwema alipita akawaona asikari; akaamuru wapigwe na baharia wa merikebu ya Sultani wetu.

Vipofu wafupi. Kiziwi mgeni. Kiroboto mkubwa. Viboko wake. Kifaru mzima. Kijakazi mzuri. Vijana wazuri. Viziwi wawivu wanane. Viboko wazito sita. Viroboto wale. Vijakazi hawa. Kiboko yule mkali. Kipofu amekufa. Nani kipofu huyu? Vijakazi wako walitwaa mwavuli wangu. Ng'ombe wamenona. Punda walishiba. Ng'ombe aliye-*konda*.

COMPARISON OF ADJECTIVES.

(*page* 114)

Malindi mji wa kale kuliko Mvita. Maneno ya watu wa Mvita sahihi kuliko maneno ya Unguja. Watu wabaya wabaya kuliko nyama. Mitende mizuri kuliko minazi. Dawa iliyo chungu. Joho hii nyeusi kuliko hii, lakini iliyo nyeusi sana ni ile. Mto huu mpana kuliko Rovuma. Mahali pale safi kuliko hapa? Furaha yangu kamili kuliko yako. Hesabu za msimamizi sahihi kuliko zile za mvuvi. Watumwa werevu kuliko msimamizi, waka mdanganya. Mzungu mkali kuliko mwashi akawapiga watumwa wote. Baruti iliyo pipani kavu kuliko sabuni iliyo kashani. Mti huu imara kuliko ule uliotiwa shimoni jana. Mtungi huu umejaa kuliko ule. Nyumba ya Abdallah kubwa kuliko yangu, lakini yangu nzuri kuliko nyumba zote nilizoziona. Njia hii ndefu kuliko ile nyumbani kwako, lakini iliyo fupi yapita shamba lako. Mti upi ulio mgumu? Jumbe thaifu kuliko wevi. Ukuni mwepesi kuliko ubau mnene. Ndizi hizi nyekundu na tamu kuliko zako. Kengele yetu iliyo ndogo nzito kuliko yao iliyo kubwa. Ndevu ya Abdallah bin Ali ndefu, lakini ile ya Suleman ndefu sana.

TO BE.

(*page* 117)

Chuo kiko mezani. Mpishi yuko karibu. Mbau ziko merikebuni. Wavuvi wako mtumbwini. Mitumbwi iko majini. Magari yako njiani. Machungwa yako pakachani. Watumwa wengi wako mjini mwako? Wako. Naliona merikebu sita jana, ziko wapi sasa? Ziko kisiwani. Iko mitumbwi karibu yao? Iko mitumbwi saba karibu sana. Msimamizi wetu yuko wapi? Yuko shambani. Watumwa wako pamoja nawe? Wako asharini. Nani yuko? Abdallah yuko. Yuko wapi Ali? Yuko nyumbani. Mfalme yuko nje.

Mimi niliye mwema. Wewe uliye mbaya. Yeye aliye thaifu. Yeye aliye mvivu. Sisi tulio wanana. Ninyi mlio wakali. Jiwe lililo kubwa. Nyumba iliyo ndogo. Tende zilizo tamu. Mtu aliye mzee. Mfalme aliye mlevi. Kipande kilicho kidogo. Kasha lililo zito. Mishale iliyo mikali. Bithaa zilizo ghali.

(page 117)

Kitabu kilichoko mezani. Mbau zilizoko merikebuni. Wavuvi walioko mtumbwini. Mitumbwi iliyoko majini. Machungwa yaliyoko mitini. Watumwa walioko mjini mwetu watakimbia wote, wakiiona bunduki iliyoko mkononi mwako. Merikebu zilizoko kisiwani zitauharibu mji ulioko upande huu wa mto. Jumbe alioko mjini mwetu. Miti iliyoko njiani.

(page 118)

Abdallah alikuwa mfalme, mimi nalikuwa mtumwa. Walikuwa mtu mwema. Alikuwa mvuvi. Walikuwa watumwa wavivu. Wazungu walikuwa watu wakali. Watu wale walikuwa weusi wote. Mwenyewe alikuwa mtu wa akili, wangine walikuwa wajinga.

Watu weusi walikuwako mwituni. Mzungu alikuwako mzingani. Bunduki yalikuwako nyumbani. Nyumba yalikuwako mtoni, mto walikuwako karibu na mlima. Mlima walikuwako kisiwana. Kisiwa chalikuwako baharini. Watu wengi walikuwako mjini, lakini watu wachache walikuwa nje ya nyumba.

(*page* 119)

Mfalme alikuwako nyumbani, watu wake walikuwako mbali. Mzungu alikuwako juu ya mwamba. Mtumbwi walikuwako karibu. Naliona watu wawili waliokuwako mlangoni pa nyumba, karibu na mtende. Mfalme alisema, ulikuwa mzee zamani, nikamwambia, wewe ulikuwa mtoto? Akaniambia nalikuwa kijana. Merikebu zalikuwako baharini, watu walikuwako mjini. Watumwa walikuwa watumishi wa Mzungu. Nilikuwako mjini nikaziona nyumba za kale zilizokuwako. Naliona watu wengi, walikuwako njiani, lakini wale wenzi wetu waliowaona walikuwako mwituni, nao haba. Watu wengi walikuwako na mfalme. Wachache walikimbia, wale waliokimbia walikuwako baadaye mjini kwetu, nikawauwa wote. Makasha makubwa matano yalikuwako nyumbani mwangu siku nyingi.

Watu waliokuwako mjini waliogopa, sisi tuliokuwako nje tukakimbia. Mfalme aliwaita wavuvi waliokuwako mtumbwini. Uliwaona watu waliokuwako? Mitumbwi mingapi iliyokuwako imezama? Mzungu alikata miti yote iliyokuwako shambani. Mfalme aliwaua wote waliokuwa watumwa wetu. Makasha yaliokuwako kwangu yalivunjwa na wevi waliokuwako baadaye mjini kwenu. Nyumba zilizokuwako zimeanguka zote. Nilivinunua vitabu vyote vilivyokuwako. Alikileta chuo kilichokuwako mezani mwangu.

IRREGULAR VERBS.

(page 122)

Wevi watano waliyakwiba makasha yaliyo kuwako nyumbani kwangu. Bithaa zilizokuwako merikebuni zalikwibwa na wavuvi. Wajakazi walikwanza kwimba. Walikwimba nyimbo nzuri nyingi. Jumbe alikwenda koga mtoni. Ndizi hazijaiva bado, zimekomaa lakini si tamu. Ulikuza watumwa wanne mwenyewe. Tutaioka mikate utakayoitaka njiani. Fetha zetu zimekwisha, hatuwezi kununua maboga yako. Embe zitakwisha ukizila sasa. Aliyeniita nani? Anayekwimba nani? Sijaisha bado. Utakwisha lini? Usiibe watu. Endeni mjini, mkaite watu watano waimbe nyimbo nyumbani kwangu. Watu wetu wamekula ndizi zote, hatukuza hatta moja. Utakufa. Atakuja kwetu. Tutakula nyama. Nyama imeliwa, aliyopewa nami. Tule, tukanywe. Usiku utakuja na watumwa watakula. Sikuzote twanywa maji tu. Jua linakuchwa.

TO HAVE.

(page 124)

Nalitaka kununua nazi zote mfalme alizokuwa nazo, lakini naona alikuwa nazo nyingi nisizozipata. Nina upanga, nawe una mkuke na ngao, tuogope nini? Mtu akiwa na fetha atakuwa mkuu. Kama mtu hana fetha hatakuwa mkuu. Nyumba yangu kubwa haina mlango. Sikuwa na nyumba zamani, sasa ninazo hizi tatu. Wevi walikwiba killa kitu tulichokuwa nacho. Mzee ana vyuo vya thamani vingi. Nitanunua vyuo vyote walivyo navyo Wazungu. Nalikuza vitabu vyote nilivyokuwa navyo mwenyewe, illa vile ulivyonipa. Ninavyo sasa nyumbani. Abdallah akifa, nitakuwa na fetha nyingi. Nitakuwa nayo mali utakayonipa. Usiponipa kitu, sitakuwa na kitu. Alijaribu kuniua nikampiga kwa upanga niliokuwa nao.

(page 125)

Hapana mtu nyumbani. Hakuna mtu anayejua kumshinda. Hapana kitu, nje. Nalitafuta kisu lakini kisu hapana. Naliona upanga mkononi mwake, nikatazama tena, hakuwa na upanga, hatta sasa hapana. Palikuwa na mtu, sasa hapana mtu.

COMPOUND TENSES.

(page 126)

Sikuwa nikienda mjini, lakini nitarudi sasa. Alikuwa akila. Sikumwona, alikuwa amekwisha kupita. Mwivi alikuwa amekwiba fetha. Ulikuwa umekisoma kitabu? Sikuwa nimekisoma. Nalikuwa nikikitazama. Wavuvi walikuwako baharini, walikuwa wameona samaki haba usiku. Vijana walikuwa wakilima shamba lao. Alikuwa ameufunga mlango. Nalikuwa nimewakata vidole. Nitakuwa nikikata mitende yao. Alikuwa akila chakula chake. Amekwisha kula. Walikuwa wakiiba nazi shambani kwangu. Watumwa walikuwa wakiniambia habari zote za wevi. Msimamizi alikuwa akienda, lakini vijakazi walikuwa wamekimbia. Nitakuwa nikitoka nyumbani. Alikuwa akiingia mlangoni. Nalikuona, ulikuwa ukimpiga kofi mtwana wangu.

DERIVATIVE VERBS.

(page 127)

Kuombea. Kuogea. Kuletea. Kujengea. Kusetea. Kuponyea. Kukokotea. Kuotea. Kuelezea. Kuonea. Kutokea. Kuondokea. Kutwekea. Kuchekea. Kulegezea. Kukosea. Kuwekea. Kusemea. Kupelekea. Kunenea. Kungojea. Kuoshea. Kuendea.

Aliniombea. Nalimletea kitabu. Walitujengea ukuta. Nitakuponyea mtumwa wako. Nalimwotea mfalme. Mzee alituelezea sauti tuliyoisikia. Nakuonea uovu. Mahali tutakapotokea. Nalimwondokea. Twalimtwekea mfalme bandera. Mpishi aliwawekea watoto chakula kingi. Nalimngojea siku nyingi. Nioshee sahani hizi. Aliiendea njia hii.

(page 128)

Kupigia. Kufikia. Kuulizia. Kuamkia. Kuumia. Kuvunjia. Kuitia. Kukamatia. Kugeukia. Kupandia. Kukusanyia. Kuvukia. Kulimia. Kukatia. Kulindia. Kukania. Kuchimbia. Kuvutia. Kufukuzia. Kumwagia. Kupungukia. Kuishia. Kukunjia. Kupatia. Kushukia. Kufishia. Kuachia. Kutazamia. Kutafutia. Kupimia. Kulipia. Kuimbia. Kusikitikia. Kusimamia. Kutupia. Kufungia. Kufutia.

Nataka unipigie mtu huyu. Nitamwulizia mpishi. Umenivunjia kisu changu. Sijui nililoitiwa. Wavu unaokamatia nyama. Wapagazi walinigeukia. Walinipandia. Mfalme aliwakusanyia watu wake wote. Siuoni mtumbwi waliouvukia. Tunamlimia mfalme. Nikatie fimbo. Alimkaniia jumbe maneno, aliyonifichia. Sitakuchimbia. Tufukuzie watumwa. Wavuvi walikuwa wakitazamia merikebu. Alikataa kunipimia njia. Wajakazi walikuwa wakimwimbia msimamizi shambani kwako, naye alikuwa akiwalipia fetha. Nakusikitikia. Mtupia mkuke. Wafungia mlango. Jumbe aliimbiwa na watu wetu. Nalitupiwa mawe na vijana. Naliachiwa shamba. Nalisikitikiwa.

(*page* 130)

Kusumbulia. Kuzalia. Kuchukulia. Kuchagulia. Kupungulia. Kusikilia. Kuzuilia. Kuamulia. Kulilia. Kununulia. Kupindulia. Kutilia. Kuvalia. Kutolea. Kupokelea. Kukatalia. Kukalia. Kusugulia. Kukimbilia. Kunyolea. Kupasulia. Kutwalia. Kuvulia. Kurarulia. Kufunulia. Kutembelea.

(*page* 130)

Tuutembelee mjini. Tufungulie mlango. Mfunulie mpishi chungu. Nalimvulia viatu vyangu. Wamenitwalia watoto wangu. Nipe shoka nipasulie mbau. Uko wapi wembe nilionyolewa. Wataka mji waukimbilie. Tusugulie meza. Wafalme hawakumkatalia haja yake. Mtu wa kwanza alimpokelea wa pili fetha. Nimekutolea fetha. Miti imeng'olewa yote. Nimeng'olewa miti yangu yote. Aliinuliwa. Mtumwa alimchinjia nyama jumbe wake. Nifungulie mlango.

(*page* 131)

Kubatilia, kubatiliwa. Kushtakia, kushtakiwa. Kukubalia, kukubaliwa. Kubadilia, kubadiliwa. Kuhubiria, kuhubiriwa. Kujibia, kujibiwa. Kuwasilia, kuwasiliwa. Kuhimilia, kuhimiliwa. Kusihia, kusihiwa. Kusadikia, kusadikiwa. Kuaminia, kuaminiwa. Kujelidia, kujelidiwa. Kubarikia, kubarikiwa. Kukirithia, kukirithiwa. Kuzabunia, kuzabuniwa. Kutakabathia, kutakabathiwa. Kudirikia, kudirikiwa. Kuathibia, kuathibiwa. Kuhitaria, kuhitariwa. Kutahiria, kutahiriwa. Kushawishia, kushawishiwa. Kukaribia, kukaribiwa. Kufarijia, kufarijiwa. Kuamuria, kuamuriwa. Kuhitimia, kuhitimiwa. Kusetiria, kusetiriwa. Kukiria, kukiriwa. Kutumainia, kutumainiwa. Kufikiria, kufikiriwa. Kusahihia, kusahihiwa. Kuwakifia, kuwakifiwa. Kutamania, kutamaniwa. Kuhulukia, kuhulukiwa. Kusulibia, kusulibiwa. Kuvinjaria, kuvinjariwa. Kulaania, kulaaniwa. Kuthubutia, kuthubutiwa. Kufarikia, kufarikiwa. Kuthalimia, kuthalimiwa. Kufawitia, kufawitiwa. Kuhinia, kuhiniwa. Kuuzulia, kuuzuliwa. Kustahilia, kustahiliwa. Kufathilia, kufathiliwa. Kutharaulia, kutharauliwa. Kuasia, kuasiwa. Kustarehea, kustarehewa. Kuhusudia, kuhusudiwa. Kutanafusia, kutanafusiwa. Kuketia, kuketiwa. Kustahimilia, kustahimiliwa. Kuhakikia, kuhakikiwa. Kusayilia, kusayiliwa. Kutahidia, kutahidiwa. Kufasiria, kufasiriwa. Kubainia, kubainiwa. Kufurahia, kufurahiwa. Kusitawia, kusitawiwa. Kutabiria, kutabiriwa. Kubashiria, kubashiriwa. Kusahaulia, kusahauliwa. Kukabithia, kukabithiwa. Kunathiria, kunathiriwa. Kumilikia, kumilikiwa. Kuthania, kuthaniwa. Kuhamia, kuhamiwa. Kuthuria, kuthuriwa. Kuaunia, kuauniwa. Kuarifia, kuarifiwa. Kuhifathia, kuhifathiwa. Kurudia, kurudiwa. Kutuhumia, kutuhumiwa. Kugharimia, kugharimiwa. Kufuturia, kufuturiwa. Kusakifia, kusakifiwa. Kurissimia, kurissimiwa. Kuhalifia, kuhalifiwa. Kukabilia, kukabiliwa. Kusamehea, kusamehewa. Kusubiria, kusubiriwa. Kudumia, kudumiwa. Kulaabia, kulaabiwa. Kuabudia, kuabudiwa. Kuhutubia, kuhutubiwa. Kuafia, kuafiwa. Kukirihia, kukirihiwa. Kusujudia, kusujudiwa. Kufidia, kufidiwa. Kutubia, kutubiwa. Kushutumia, kushutumiwa. Kuhuia, kuhuiwa. Kutilifia, kutilifiwa. Kukinaia, kukinaiwa. Kufilisia, kufilisiwa. Kufitinia, kufitiniwa. Kusakia, kusakiwa. Kudaia, kudaiwa. Kuruzukia, kuruzukiwa. Kuthaminia, kuthamaniwa. Kuhadithia, kuhadithiwa. Kushuhudia, kushuhudiwa. Kusafiria, kusafiriwa. Kutadarikia, kutadarikiwa. Kujeruhia, kujeruhiwa. Kustaajabia, kustaajabiwa.

page 132.

Shoka la kupasulia kuni. Neno la kumjibia. Fimbo ya kupigia mbwa. Upepo ulizivumia mbali karatasi. Watu wataka miti ya kujengea. Sioni mtu wa kuitia. Nina wapagazi wa kunichukulia. Naona mahali pa kupandia. Chungu cha kupikia viazi. Walikatia mbali mlingote. Watumwa wanayo majembe ya kulimia. Kamba ya kuvutia gari. Jumbe aliwafukuzia mbali adui wake. Sioni maneno ya kuelezea maana yangu. Uko wapi mkufu wa kumfungia? Ndege walirukia mbali. Nipe misomari mirefu ya kuzifungia mbau. Tuwaulie mbali wote. Sukumia mbali jiwe. Kitanda cha kupumzikia. Lete maji ya kuzioshea sahani. Nina nguo ya kuzifutia baadaye.

page 133.

Kushtakiana. Kujibiana. Kusumbuana. Kuitana. Kudanganyana. Kuponyana. Kulindana. Kuogopana. Kulishana. Kuonana. Kusameheana. Kuchukiana. Kusayidiana. Kuagana. Kukutana. Kupendezana. Kusifiana. Kutharauliana. Kufundishana. Kuambiana.

page 134.

Kufutika. Kuosheka. Kutumika. Kufunuka. Kutatuka. Kupasuka. Kumwagika. Kutikisika. Kushoneka. Kutafutika. Kutharaulika. Kutawanyika. Kuvutika. Kuinuka. Kushuka. Kupitika. Kusagika. Kusahaulika. Kukunjika. Kununulika. Kukubalika. Kusumbuka.

page 136.

1. Kuchukiza. Kujaza. Kuzoeza. Kufanyiza. Kuingiza. Kugombeza. Kukweza. Kushangaza. Kutuliza. Kuchukuza. Kugeuza. Kueleza. Kuokoza. Kukataza. Kukimbiza. Kulekeza. Kutimiza. Kupenyeza. Kuregeza. Kukuza. Kupoza. Kusikiliza. Kupoteza. Kujongeza. Kusogeza. Kŭlipiza. Kutegemeza. Kueneza. Kukwaza. Kuliza.

SWAHILI EXERCISES: KEY.

2. Kuwezesha. Kujumlisha. Kubadilisha Kukaribisha. Kupandisha. Kuinamisha. Kupofusha. Kuvumisha. Kukosesha. Kusumbusha. Kupatanisha. Kukomesha. Kukutanisha. Kulinganisha. Kusulibisha. Kufurahisha. Kupiganisha. Kushibisha. Kukopesha. Kurudisha. Kuinamisha. Kukwamisha. Kuzibisha. Kuthubutisha. Kutatanisha. Kuwasilisha. Kustarehesha. Kuthanisha. Kusafirisha. Kutaajabisha.

3. Kuepusha. Kutesa. Kutaabisha. Kuondosha. Kuamsha. Kupofusha. Kuchemsha. Kutakasa. Kuvusha. Kuokoa. Kuchesha. Kukausha. Kuangusha. Kukumbusha. Kuwasha. Kurusha. Kunyosha. Kutikisa. Kufingirisha. Kutosa. Kukasirisha. Kuzungusha.

Kazi yetu imekwisha. Sasa twajua kuandika Kiswahili kama mtu aliyezaliwa katika Unguja. Watu watatutaajabia. Mtu akituuliza maulizo twajua maneno yaliyo sahihi ya kumjibia.

November, 1881.

A CLASSIFIED LIST

OF

EDUCATIONAL WORKS

PUBLISHED BY

GEORGE BELL & SONS.

Full Catalogues will be sent post free on application.

BIBLIOTHECA CLASSICA.

A Series of Greek and Latin Authors, with English Notes, edited by eminent Scholars. 8vo.

Æschylus. By F. A. Paley, M.A. 18s.
Cicero's Orations. By G. Long, M.A. 4 vols. 16s., 14s., 16s., 18s.
Demosthenes. By R. Whiston, M.A. 2 vols. 16s. each.
Euripides. By F. A. Paley, M.A. 3 vols. 16s. each.
Homer. By F. A. Paley, M.A. Vol. I. 12s.; Vol. II. 14s.
Herodotus. By Rev. J. W. Blakesley, B.D. 2 vols. 32s.
Hesiod. By F. A. Paley, M.A. 10s. 6d.
Horace. By Rev. A. J. Macleane, M.A. 18s.
Juvenal and Persius. By Rev. A. J. Macleane, M.A. 12s.
Plato. By W. H. Thompson, D.D. 2 vols. 7s. 6d. each.
Sophocles. Vol. I. By Rev. F. H. Blaydes, M.A. 18s.
———— Vol. II. Philoctetes. Electra. Ajax and Trachiniæ. By F. A. Paley, M.A. 12s.
Tacitus: The Annals. By the Rev. P. Frost. 15s.
Terence. By E. St. J. Parry, M.A. 18s.
Virgil. By J. Conington, M.A. 3 vols. 14s. each.
An Atlas of Classical Geography; Twenty-four Maps. By W. Hughes and George Long, M.A. New edition, with coloured outlines. Imperial 8vo. 12s. 6d.

Uniform with above.

A Complete Latin Grammar. By J. W. Donaldson, D.D. 3rd Edition. 14s.

GRAMMAR-SCHOOL CLASSICS.

A Series of Greek and Latin Authors, with English Notes. Fcap. 8vo.

Cæsar: De Bello Gallico. By George Long, M.A. 5s. 6d.
———— Books I.–III. For Junior Classes. By G. Long, M.A. 2s. 6d.
Catullus, Tibullus, and Propertius. Selected Poems. With Life. By Rev. A. H. Wratislaw. 3s. 6d.

Cicero: De Senectute, De Amicitia, and Select Epistles. By George Long, M.A. 4s. 6d.
Cornelius Nepos. By Rev. J. F. Macmichael. 2s. 6d.
Homer: Iliad. Books I.-XII. By F. A. Paley, M.A. 6s. 6d.
Horace. With Life. By A. J. Macleane, M.A. 6s. 6d. [In 2 parts. 3s. 6d. each.]
Juvenal: Sixteen Satires. By H. Prior, M.A. 4s. 6d.
Martial: Select Epigrams. With Life. By F. A. Paley, M.A. 6s. 6d.
Ovid: the Fasti. By F. A. Paley, M.A. 5s.
Sallust: Catilina and Jugurtha. With Life. By G. Long, M.A. 5s.
Tacitus: Germania and Agricola. By Rev. P. Frost. 3s. 6d.
Virgil: Bucolics, Georgics, and Æneid, Books I.-IV. Abridged from Professor Conington's Edition. 5s. 6d.—Æneid, Books V.-XII. 5s. 6d. Also in 9 separate Volumes, 1s. 6d. each.
Xenophon: The Anabasis. With Life. By Rev. J. F. Macmichael. 5s. Also in 4 separate volumes, 1s. 6d. each.
——— The Cyropædia. By G. M. Gorham, M.A. 6s.
——— Memorabilia. By Percival Frost, M.A. 4s. 6d.
A Grammar-School Atlas of Classical Geography, containing Ten selected Maps. Imperial 8vo. 5s.

Uniform with the Series.

The New Testament, in Greek. With English Notes, &c. By Rev. J. F. Macmichael. 7s. 6d.

CAMBRIDGE GREEK AND LATIN TEXTS.

Æschylus. By F. A. Paley, M.A. 3s.
Cæsar: De Bello Gallico. By G. Long, M.A. 2s.
Cicero: De Senectute et de Amicitia, et Epistolæ Selectæ. By G. Long, M.A. 1s. 6d.
Ciceronis Orationes. Vol. I. (in Verrem.) By G. Long, M.A. 3s. 6d.
Euripides. By F. A. Paley, M.A. 3 vols. 3s. 6d. each.
Herodotus. By J. G. Blakesley, B.D. 2 vols. 7s.
Homeri Ilias. I.-XII. By F. A. Paley, M.A. 2s. 6d.
Horatius. By A. J. Macleane, M.A. 2s. 6d.
Juvenal et Persius. By A. J. Macleane, M.A. 1s. 6d.
Lucretius. By H. A. J. Munro, M.A. 2s. 6d.
Sallusti Crispi Catilina et Jugurtha. By G. Long, M.A. 1s. 6d.
Sophocles. By F. A. Paley, M.A. [*In the press.*
Terenti Comœdiæ. By W. Wagner, Ph.D. 3s.
Thucydides. By J. G. Donaldson, D.D. 2 vols. 7s.
Virgilius. By J. Conington, M.A. 3s. 6d.
Xenophontis Expeditio Cyri. By J. F. Macmichael, B.A. 2s. 6d.
Novum Testamentum Græcum. By F. H. Scrivener, M.A. 4s. 6d. An edition with wide margin for notes, half bound, 12s.

CAMBRIDGE TEXTS WITH NOTES.

A Selection of the most usually read of the Greek and Latin Authors, Annotated for Schools. Fcap. 8vo. 1s. 6d. each., with exceptions.

Euripides. Alcestis.—Medea.—Hippolytus.—Hecuba.—Bacchæ. Ion. 2s.—Orestes.—Phoenissæ.—Troades. By F. A. Paley, M.A.
Æschylus. Prometheus Vinctus.—Septem contra Thebas.—Agamemnon.—Persæ.—Eumenides. By F. A. Paley, M.A.
Sophocles. Œdipus Tyrannus.—Œdipus Coloneus.—Antigone. By F. A. Paley, M.A.
Homer. Iliad. Book I. By F. A. Paley, M.A. 1s.
Cicero's De Senectute—De Amicitia and Epistolæ Selectæ. By G. Long, M.A.
Ovid. Selections. By A. J. Macleane, M.A.
Others in preparation.

PUBLIC SCHOOL SERIES.

A Series of Classical Texts, annotated by well-known Scholars. Cr. 8vo.

Aristophanes. The Peace. By F. A. Paley, M.A. 4s. 6d.
———— The Acharnians. By F. A. Paley, M.A. 4s. 6d.
———— The Frogs. By F. A. Paley, M.A. 4s. 6d.
Cicero. The Letters to Atticus. Bk. I. By A. Pretor, M.A. 4s. 6d.
Demosthenes de Falsa Legatione. By R. Shilleto, M.A. 6s.
———— The Law of Leptines. By B. W. Beatson, M.A. 3s. 6d.
Plato. The Apology of Socrates and Crito. By W. Wagner, Ph.D. 6th Edition. 4s. 6d.
———— The Phædo. 6th Edition. By W. Wagner, Ph.D. 5s. 6d.
———— The Protagoras. 3rd Edition. By W. Wayte, M.A. 4s. 6d.
———— The Euthyphro. 2nd edition. By G. H. Wells. 3s.
———— The Euthydemus. By G. H. Wells. 4s.
———— The Republic. By G. H. Wells. [*Preparing.*
Plautus. The Aulularia. By W. Wagner, Ph.D. 2nd edition. 4s. 6d.
———— Trinummus. By W. Wagner, Ph.D. 2nd edition. 4s. 6d.
———— The Menaechmei. By W. Wagner, Ph.D. 4s. 6d.
Sophoclis Trachiniæ. By A. Pretor, M.A. 4s. 6d.
Terence. By W. Wagner, Ph.D. 10s. 6d.
Theocritus. By F. A. Paley, M.A. 4s. 6d.
Others in preparation.

CRITICAL AND ANNOTATED EDITIONS.

Ætna. By H. A. J. Munro, M.A. 3s. 6d.
Aristophanis Comœdiæ. By H. A. Holden, LL.D. 8vo. 2 vols. 23s. 6d. Plays sold separately.
———— Pax. By F. A. Paley, M.A. Fcap. 8vo. 4s. 6d.
Catullus. By H. A. J. Munro, M.A. 7s. 6d.
Corpus Poetarum Catinorum. Edited by Walker. 1 vol. 8vo. 18s.
Horace. Quinti Horatii Flacci Opera. By H. A. J. Munro, M.A. Large 8vo. 1l. 1s.
Livy. The first five Books. By J. Prendeville. 12mo. roan, 5s. Or Books I.-III. 3s. 6d. IV. and V. 3s. 6d.

Lucretius. Titi Lucretii Cari de Rerum Natura Libri Sex. With a Translation and Notes. By H. A. J. Munro, M.A. 2 vols. 8vo. Vol. I. Text. (New Edition, Preparing.) Vol. II. Translation. (Sold separately.)

Ovid. P. Ovidii Nasonis Heroides XIV. By A. Palmer, M.A. 8vo. 6s.

Propertius. Sex Aurelii Propertii Carmina. By F. A. Paley, M.A. 8vo. Cloth, 9s.

Sex. Propertii Elegiarum. Lib. IV. By A. Palmer. Fcap. 8vo. 5s.

Sophocles. The Ajax. By C. E. Palmer, M.A. 4s. 6d.

Thucydides. The History of the Peloponnesian War. By Richard Shilleto, M.A. Book I. 8vo. 6s. 6d. Book II. 8vo. 5s. 6d.

LATIN AND GREEK CLASS-BOOKS.

Auxilia Latina. A Series of Progressive Latin Exercises. By M. J. B. Baddeley, M.A. Fcap. 8vo. Part I. Accidence. 1s. 6d. Part II. 3rd Edition, 2s. Key, 2s. 6d.

Latin Prose Lessons. By Prof. Church, M.A. 6th Edit. Fcap. 8vo. 2s. 6d.

Latin Exercises and Grammar Papers. By T. Collins, M.A. 3rd Edition. Fcap. 8vo. 2s. 6d.

Unseen Papers in Prose and Verse. With Examination Questions. By T. Collins, M.A. 2nd edition. Fcap. 8vo. 2s. 6d.

Analytical Latin Exercises. By C. P. Mason, B.A. 3rd Edit. 3s. 6d.

Scala Græca: a Series of Elementary Greek Exercises. By Rev. J. W. Davis, M.A., and R. W. Baddeley, M.A. 3rd Edition. Fcap. 8vo. 2s. 6d.

Greek Verse Composition. By G. Preston, M.A. Crown 8vo. 4s. 6d.

BY THE REV. P. FROST, M.A., ST. JOHN'S COLLEGE, CAMBRIDGE.

Eclogæ Latinæ; or, First Latin Reading-Book, with English Notes and a Dictionary. New Edition. Fcap. 8vo. 2s. 6d.

Materials for Latin Prose Composition. New Edition. Fcap. 8vo. 2s. 6d. Key, 4s.

A Latin Verse-Book. An Introductory Work on Hexameters and Pentameters. New Edition. Fcap. 8vo. 3s. Key, 5s.

Analecta Græca Minora, with Introductory Sentences, English Notes, and a Dictionary. New Edition. Fcap. 8vo. 3s. 6d.

Materials for Greek Prose Composition. New Edit. Fcap. 8vo. 3s. 6d. Key, 5s.

Florilegium Poeticum. Elegiac Extracts from Ovid and Tibullus. New Edition. With Notes. Fcap. 8vo. 3s.

BY THE REV. F. E. GRETTON.

A First Cheque-book for Latin Verse-makers. 1s. 6d.

A Latin Version for Masters. 2s. 6d.

Reddenda; or Passages with Parallel Hints for Translation into Latin Prose and Verse. Crown 8vo. 4s. 6d.

Reddenda Reddita (see next page).

BY H. A. HOLDEN, LL.D.

Foliorum Silvula. Part I. Passages for Translation into Latin Elegiac and Heroic Verse. 9th Edition. Post 8vo. 7s. 6d.

———— Part II. Select Passages for Translation into Latin Lyric and Comic Iambic Verse. 3rd Edition. Post 8vo. 5s.

———— Part III. Select Passages for Translation into Greek Verse. 3rd Edition. Post 8vo. 8s.

Folia Silvulæ, sive Eclogæ Poetarum Anglicorum in Latinum et Græcum conversæ. 8vo. Vol. I. 10s. 6d. Vol. II. 12s.

Foliorum Centuriæ. Select Passages for Translation into Latin and Greek Prose. 7th Edition. Post 8vo. 8s.

TRANSLATIONS, SELECTIONS, &c.

*** Many of the following books are well adapted for School Prizes.

Æschylus. Translated into English Prose by F. A. Paley, M.A. 2nd Edition. 8vo. 7s. 6d.
———— Translated into English Verse by Anna Swanwick. Post 8vo. 5s.
———— Folio Edition, with 33 Illustrations after Flaxman. 2l. 2s.

Anthologia Græca. A Selection of Choice Greek Poetry, with Notes. By F. St. John Thackeray. *4th and Cheaper Edition.* 16mo. 4s. 6d.

Anthologia Latina. A Selection of Choice Latin Poetry, from Nævius to Boëthius, with Notes. By Rev. F. St. John Thackeray. Revised and Cheaper Edition. 16mo. 4s. 6d.

Horace. The Odes and Carmen Sæculare. In English Verse by J. Conington, M.A. 8th edition: Fcap. 8vo. 5s. 6d.
———— The Satires and Epistles. In English Verse by J. Conington, M.A. 5th edition. 6s. 6d.
———— Illustrated from Antique Gems by C. W. King, M.A. The text revised with Introduction by H. A. J. Munro, M.A. Large 8vo. 1l. 1s.

Horace's Odes. Englished and Imitated by various hands. Edited by C. W. F. Cooper. Crown 8vo. 6s. 6d.

Mvsæ Etonenses, sive Carminvm Etonæ Conditorvm Delectvs. By Richard Okes. 2 vols. 8vo. 15s.

Propertius. Verse translations from Book V., with revised Latin Text. By F. A. Paley, M.A. Fcap. 8vo. 3s.

Plato. Gorgias. Translated by E. M. Cope, M.A. 8vo. 7s.
———— Philebus. Translated by F. A. Paley, M.A. Small 8vo. 4s.
———— Theætetus. Translated by F. A. Paley, M.A. Small 8vo. 4s.
———— Analysis and Index of the Dialogues. By Dr. Day. Post 8vo. 5s.

Reddenda Reddita: Passages from English Poetry, with a Latin Verse Translation. By F. E. Gretton. Crown 8vo. 6s.

Sabrinæ Corolla in hortulis Regiæ Scholæ Salopiensis contexuerunt tres viri floribus legendis. Editio tertia. 8vo. 8s. 6d.

Sertum Carthusianum Floribus trium Seculorum Contextum. By W. H. Brown. 8vo. 14s.

Theocritus. In English Verse, by C. S. Calverley, M.A. Crown 8vo. [*New Edition, Preparing.*]

Translations into English and Latin. By C. S. Calverley, M.A. Post 8vo. 7s. 6d.
———— By R. C. Jebb, M.A.; H. Jackson, M.A., and W. E. Currey, M.A. Crown 8vo. 8s.
———— *into* Greek and Latin Verse. By R. C. Jebb. 4to. cloth gilt. 10s. 6d.

Between Whiles. Translations by B. H. Kennedy. Crown 8vo.

REFERENCE VOLUMES.

A Latin Grammar. By Albert Harkness. Post 8vo. 6s.
—— By T. H. Key, M.A. 6th Thousand. Post 8vo. 8s.
A Short Latin Grammar for Schools. By T. H. Key, M.A., F.R.S. 14th Edition. Post 8vo. 3s. 6d.
A Guide to the Choice of Classical Books. By J. B. Mayor, M.A. Revised Edition. Crown 8vo. 3s.
The Theatre of the Greeks. By J. W. Donaldson, D.D. 8th Edition. Post 8vo. 5s.
Keightley's Mythology of Greece and Italy. 4th Edition. 5s.
A Dictionary of Latin and Greek Quotations. By H. T. Riley. Post 8vo. 5s. With Index Verborum, 6s.
A History of Roman Literature. By W. S. Teuffel, Professor at the University of Tübingen. By W. Wagner, Ph.D. 2 vols. Demy 8vo. 21s.
Student's Guide to the University of Cambridge. 4th Edition revised. Fcap. 8vo. Part 1, 2s. 6d.; Parts 2 to 6, 1s. each.

CLASSICAL TABLES.

Latin Accidence. By the Rev. P. Frost, M.A. 1s.
Latin Versification. 1s.
Notabilia Quædam; or the Principal Tenses of most of the Irregular Greek Verbs and Elementary Greek, Latin, and French Construction. New edition. 1s.
Richmond Rules for the Ovidian Distich, &c. By J. Tate, M.A. 1s.
The Principles of Latin Syntax. 1s.
Greek Verbs. A Catalogue of Verbs, Irregular and Defective; their leading formations, tenses, and inflexions, with Paradigms for conjugation, Rules for formation of tenses, &c. &c. By J. S. Baird, T.C.D. 2s. 6d.
Greek Accents (Notes on). By A. Barry, D.D. New Edition. 1s.
Homeric Dialect. Its Leading Forms and Peculiarities. By J. S. Baird, T.C.D. New edition, by W. G. Rutherford. 1s.
Greek Accidence. By the Rev. P. Frost, M.A. New Edition. 1s.

CAMBRIDGE MATHEMATICAL SERIES.

Whitworth's Choice and Chance. 3rd Edition. Crown 8vo. 6s.
McDowell's Exercises on Euclid and in Modern Geometry. 3rd Edition. 6s.
Vyvyan's Trigonometry. Sewed.
Taylor's Geometry of Conics. Elementary. 3rd Edition. 4s. 6d.
Aldis's Solid Geometry. 3rd Edition. 6s.
Garnett's Elementary Dynamics. 2nd Edition. 6s.
—— Heat, an Elementary Treatise. 2nd Edition. 3s. 6d.
Walton's Elementary Mechanics (Problems in). 2nd Edition. 6s.

CAMBRIDGE SCHOOL AND COLLEGE TEXT-BOOKS.

A Series of Elementary Treatises for the use of Students in the Universities, Schools, and Candidates for the Public Examinations. Fcap. 8vo.

Arithmetic. By Rev. C. Elsee, M.A. Fcap. 8vo. 10th Edit. 3s. 6d.
Algebra. By the Rev. C. Elsee, M.A. 6th Edit. 4s.
Arithmetic. By A. Wrigley, M.A. 3s. 6d.
―――― A Progressive Course of Examples. With Answers. By J. Watson, M.A. 5th Edition. 2s. 6d.
Algebra. Progressive Course of Examples. By Rev. W. F. M'Michael, M.A., and R. Prowde Smith, M.A. 2nd Edition. 3s. 6d. With Answers. 4s. 6d.
Plane Astronomy, An Introduction to. By P. T. Main, M.A. 4th Edition. 4s.
Conic Sections treated Geometrically. By W. H. Besant, M.A. 4th Edition. 4s. 6d.
Elementary Conic Sections treated Geometrically. By W. H. Besant, M.A. [In the Press.
Statics, Elementary. By Rev. H. Goodwin, D.D. 2nd Edit. 3s.
Hydrostatics, Elementary. By W. H. Besant, M.A. 10th Edit. 4s.
Mensuration, An Elementary Treatise on. By B. T. Moore, M.A. 6s.
Newton's Principia, The First Three Sections of, with an Appendix; and the Ninth and Eleventh Sections. By J. H. Evans, M.A. 5th Edition, by P. T. Main, M.A. 4s.
Trigonometry, Elementary. By T. P. Hudson, M.A. 3s. 6d.
Optics, Geometrical. With Answers. By W. S. Aldis, M.A. 3s. 6d.
Analytical Geometry for Schools. By T. G. Vyvyan. 3rd Edit. 4s. 6d.
Greek Testament, Companion to the. By A. C. Barrett, A.M. 4th Edition, revised. Fcap. 8vo. 5s.
Book of Common Prayer, An Historical and Explanatory Treatise on the. By W. G. Humphry, B.D. 6th Edition. Fcap. 8vo. 4s. 6d.
Music, Text-book of. By H. C. Banister. 9th Edit. revised. 5s.
―――― Concise History of. By Rev. H. G. Bonavia Hunt, B. Mus. Oxon. 5th Edition revised. 3s. 6d.

ARITHMETIC AND ALGEBRA.
See foregoing Series.

GEOMETRY AND EUCLID.

Text-Book of Geometry. By T. S. Aldis, M.A. Small 8vo. 4s. 6d. Part I. 2s. 6d. Part II. 2s.
The Elements of Euclid. By H. J. Hose. Fcap. 8vo. 4s. 6d. Exercises separately, 1s.
―――― The First Six Books, with Commentary by Dr. Lardner. 10th Edition. 8vo. 6s.
―――― The First Two Books explained to Beginners. By C. Mason, B.A. 2nd Edition. Fcap 8vo. 2s. 6d.

The Enunciations and Figures to Euclid's Elements. By Rev.
J. Brasse, D.D. New Edition. Fcap. 8vo. 1s. On Cards, in case, 5s. 6d.
Without the Figures, 6d.
Exercises on Euclid and in Modern Geometry. By J. McDowell,
B.A. Crown 8vo. 3rd Edition revised. 6s.
Geometrical Conic Sections. By W. H. Besant, M.A. 4th Edit.
4s. 6d.
Elementary Geometrical Conic Sections. By W. H. Besant,
M.A. [In the Press.
Elementary Geometry of Conics. By C. Taylor, M.A. 3rd Edit.
8vo. 4s. 6d.
An Introduction to Ancient and Modern Geometry of Conics.
By C. Taylor, M.A. 8vo. 15s.
Solutions of Geometrical Problems, proposed at St. John's
College from 1830 to 1846. By T. Gaskin, M.A. 8vo. 12s.

TRIGONOMETRY.

Trigonometry, Introduction to Plane. By Rev. T. G. Vyvyan,
Charterhouse. Cr. 8vo. Sewed.
Elementary Trigonometry. By T. P. Hudson, M.A. 3s. 6d.
An Elementary Treatise on Mensuration. By B. T. Moore,
M.A. 5s.

ANALYTICAL GEOMETRY
AND DIFFERENTIAL CALCULUS.

An Introduction to Analytical Plane Geometry. By W. P.
Turnbull, M.A. 8vo. 12s.
Problems on the Principles of Plane Co-ordinate Geometry.
By W. Walton, M.A. 8vo. 16s.
Trilinear Co-ordinates, and Modern Analytical Geometry of
Two Dimensions. By W. A. Whitworth, M.A. 8vo. 16s.
An Elementary Treatise on Solid Geometry. By W. S. Aldis,
M.A. 2nd Edition revised. 8vo. 8s.
Elementary Treatise on the Differential Calculus. By M.
O'Brien, M.A. 8vo. 10s. 6d.
Elliptic Functions, Elementary Treatise on. By A. Cayley, M.A.
Demy 8vo. 15s.

MECHANICS & NATURAL PHILOSOPHY.

Statics, Elementary. By H. Goodwin, D.D. Fcap. 8vo. 2nd
Edition. 3s.
Dynamics, A Treatise on Elementary. By W. Garnett, M.A.
2nd Edition. Crown 8vo. 6s.
Elementary Mechanics, Problems in. By W. Walton, M.A. New
Edition. Crown 8vo. 6s.
Theoretical Mechanics, Problems in. By W. Walton. 2nd Edit.
revised and enlarged. Demy 8vo. 16s.

Hydrostatics. By W. H. Besant, M.A. Fcap. 8vo. 10th Edition. 4s.
Hydromechanics, A Treatise on. By W. H. Besant, M.A. 8vo. New Edition revised. 10s. 6d.
Dynamics of a Particle, A Treatise on the. By W. H. Besant, M.A. [*Preparing*.
Optics, Geometrical. By W. S. Aldis, M.A. Fcap. 8vo. 3s. 6d.
Double Refraction, A Chapter on Fresnel's Theory of. By W. S. Aldis, M.A. 8vo. 2s.
Heat, An Elementary Treatise on. By W. Garnett, M.A. Crown 8vo. 2nd Edition revised. 3s. 6d.
Newton's Principia, The First Three Sections of, with an Appendix; and the Ninth and Eleventh Sections. By J. H. Evans, M.A. 5th Edition. Edited by P. T. Main, M.A. 4s.
Astronomy, An Introduction to Plane. By P. T. Main, M.A. Fcap. 8vo. cloth. 4s.
Astronomy, Practical and Spherical. By R. Main, M.A. 8vo. 14s.
Astronomy, Elementary Chapters on, from the 'Astronomic Physique' of Biot. By H. Goodwin, D.D. 8vo. 3s. 6d.
Pure Mathematics and Natural Philosophy, A Compendium of Facts and Formulæ in. By G. R. Smalley. Fcap. 8vo. 3s. 6d.
Elementary Course of Mathematics. By H. Goodwin, D.D. 6th Edition. 8vo. 16s.
Problems and Examples, adapted to the 'Elementary Course of Mathematics.' 3rd Edition. 8vo. 5s.
Solutions of Goodwin's Collection of Problems and Examples. By W. W. Hutt, M.A. 3rd Edition, revised and enlarged. 8vo. 9s.
Pure Mathematics, Elementary Examples in. By J. Taylor. 8vo. 7s. 6d.
Mechanics of Construction. With numerous Examples. By S. Fenwick, F.R.A.S. 8vo. 12s.
Pure and Applied Calculation, Notes on the Principles of. By Rev. J. Challis, M.A. Demy 8vo. 15s.
Physics, The Mathematical Principle of. By Rev. J. Challis, M.A. Demy 8vo. 5s.

TECHNOLOGICAL HANDBOOKS.

Edited by H. Trueman Wood, Secretary of the Society of Arts.

1. Dyeing and Tissue Printing. By W. Crookes, F.R.S. [*In the press*.
2. Iron and Steel. By Prof. A. K. Huntington, of King's College. [*Preparing*.
3. Cotton Manufacture. By Richard Marsden, Esq., of Manchester. [*Preparing*.
4. Telegraphs and Telephones. By W. H. Preece, F.R.S. [*Preparing*.
5. Glass Manufacture. By Henry Chance, M.A.; H. Powell, B.A. and John Hopkinson, M.A., LL.D., F.R.S.

HISTORY, TOPOGRAPHY, &c.

Rome and the Campagna. By R. Burn, M.A. With 85 Engravings and 26 Maps and Plans. With Appendix. 4to. 3l. 3s.

Old Rome. A Handbook for Travellers. By R. Burn, M.A. With Maps and Plans. Demy 8vo. 10s. 6d.

Modern Europe. By Dr. T. H. Dyer. 2nd Edition, revised and continued. 5 vols. Demy 8vo. 2l. 12s. 6d.

The History of the Kings of Rome. By Dr. T. H. Dyer. 8vo. 16s.

The History of Pompeii: its Buildings and Antiquities. By T. H. Dyer. 3rd Edition, brought down to 1874. Post 8vo. 7s. 6d.

Ancient Athens: its History, Topography, and Remains. By T. H. Dyer. Super-royal 8vo. Cloth. 1l. 5s.

The Decline of the Roman Republic. By G. Long. 5 vols. 8vo. 14s. each.

A History of England during the Early and Middle Ages. By C. H. Pearson, M.A. 2nd Edition revised and enlarged. 8vo. Vol. I. 16s. Vol. II. 14s.

Historical Maps of England. By C. H. Pearson. Folio. 2nd Edition revised. 31s. 6d.

History of England, 1800–15. By Harriet Martineau, with new and copious Index. 1 vol. 3s. 6d.

History of the Thirty Years' Peace, 1815–46. By Harriet Martineau. 4 vols. 3s. 6d. each.

A Practical Synopsis of English History. By A. Bowes. 4th Edition. 8vo. 2s.

Student's Text-Book of English and General History. By D. Beale. Crown 8vo. 2s. 6d.

Lives of the Queens of England. By A. Strickland. Library Edition, 8 vols. 7s. 6d. each. Cheaper Edition, 6 vols. 5s. each. Abridged Edition, 1 vol. 6s. 6d.

Eginhard's Life of Karl the Great (Charlemagne). Translated with Notes, by W. Glaister, M.A., B.C.L. Crown 8vo. 4s. 6d.

Outlines of Indian History. By A. W. Hughes. Small post 8vo. 3s. 6d.

The Elements of General History. By Prof. Tytler. New Edition, brought down to 1874. Small post 8vo. 3s. 6d.

ATLASES.

An Atlas of Classical Geography. 24 Maps. By W. Hughes and G. Long, M.A. New Edition. Imperial 8vo. 12s. 6d.

A Grammar-School Atlas of Classical Geography. Ten Maps selected from the above. New Edition. Imperial 8vo. 5s.

First Classical Maps. By the Rev. J. Tate, M.A. 3rd Edition. Imperial 8vo. 7s. 6d.

Standard Library Atlas of Classical Geography. Imp. 8vo. 7s. 6d.

PHILOLOGY.

**WEBSTER'S DICTIONARY OF THE ENGLISH LAN-
GUAGE.** With Dr. Mahn's Etymology. 1 vol., 1628 Pages, 3000 Illustrations. 21s. With Appendices and 70 additional pages of Illustrations, 1919 Pages, 31s. 6d.
'THE BEST PRACTICAL ENGLISH DICTIONARY EXTANT.'—*Quarterly Review*, 1873.
Prospectuses, with specimen pages, post free on application.

New Dictionary of the English Language. Combining Explanation with Etymology, and copiously illustrated by Quotations from the best Authorities. By Dr. Richardson. New Edition, with a Supplement. 2 vols. 4to. 4l. 14s. 6d.; half russia, 5l. 15s. 6d.; russia, 6l. 12s. Supplement separately. 4to. 12s.
An 8vo. Edit. without the Quotations, 15s.; half russia, 20s.; russia, 24s.

Supplementary English Glossary. Containing 12,000 words and meanings occurring in English Literature, not found in any other Dictionary. By T. L. O. Davies. Demy 8vo. 16s.

Dictionary of Corrupted Words. By Rev. A. S. Palmer. [*In the press.*

Brief History of the English Language. By Prof. James Hadley, LL.D., Yale College. Fcap. 8vo. 1s.

The Elements of the English Language. By E. Adams, Ph.D. 15th Edition. Post 8vo. 4s. 6d.

Philological Essays. By T. H. Key, M.A., F.R.S. 8vo. 10s. 6d.

Language, its Origin and Development. By T. H. Key, M.A., F.R.S. 8vo. 14s.

Synonyms and Antonyms of the English Language. By Archdeacon Smith. 2nd Edition. Post 8vo. 5s.

Synonyms Discriminated. By Archdeacon Smith. Demy 8vo. 16s.

Bible English. By T. L. O. Davies. 5s.

The Queen's English. A Manual of Idiom and Usage. By the late Dean Alford. 5th Edition. Fcap. 8vo. 5s.

Etymological Glossary of nearly 2500 English Words derived from the Greek. By the Rev. E. J. Boyce. Fcap. 8vo. 3s. 6d.

A Syriac Grammar. By G. Phillips, D.D. 3rd Edition, enlarged. 8vo. 7s. 6d.

A Grammar of the Arabic Language. By Rev. W. J. Beaumont, M.A. 12mo. 7s.

DIVINITY, MORAL PHILOSOPHY, &c.

Novum Testamentum Græcum, Textus Stephanici, 1550. By F. H. Scrivener, A.M., LL.D. New Edition. 16mo. 4s. 6d. Also on Writing Paper, with Wide Margin. Half-bound. 12s.

By the same Author.

Codex Bezæ Cantabrigiensis. 4to. 26s.

A Full Collation of the Codex Sinaiticus with the Received Text of the New Testament, with Critical Introduction. 2nd Edition, revised. Fcap. 8vo. 5s.

A Plain Introduction to the Criticism of the New Testament. With Forty Facsimiles from Ancient Manuscripts. 2nd Edition. 8vo. 18s.

Six Lectures **on the Text of the New Testament.** For English Readers. Crown 8vo. 6s.

The New Testament for English Readers. By the late H. Alford, D.D. Vol. I. Part I. 3rd Edit. 12s. Vol. I. Part II. 2nd Edit. 10s. 6d. Vol. II. Part I. 2nd Edit. 16s. Vol. II. Part II. 2nd Edit. 16s.

The Greek Testament. By the late H. Alford, D.D. Vol. I. 6th Edit. 1l. 8s. Vol. II. 6th Edit. 1l. 4s. Vol. III. 5th Edit. 18s. Vol. IV. Part I. 4th Edit. 18s. Vol. IV. Part II. 4th Edit. 14s. Vol. IV. 1l. 12s.

Companion to the Greek Testament. By A. C. Barrett, M.A. 4th Edition, revised. Fcap. 8vo. 5s.

The Book of Psalms. A New Translation, with Introductions, &c. By the Very Rev. J. J. Stewart Perowne, D.D. 8vo. Vol. I. 4th Edition, 18s. Vol. II. 4th Edit. 16s.

——— Abridged for Schools. 3rd Edition. Crown 8vo. 10s. 6d.

History of the Articles of Religion. By C. H. Hardwick. 3rd Edition. Post 8vo. 5s.

History of the Creeds. By J. R. Lumby, D.D. 2nd Edition. Crown 8vo. 7s. 6d.

Pearson on the Creed. Carefully printed from an early edition. With Analysis and Index by E. Walford, M.A. Post 8vo. 5s.

An Historical and Explanatory Treatise on the Book of Common Prayer. By Rev. W. G. Humphry, B.D. 6th Edition, enlarged. Small post 8vo. 4s. 6d.

The New Table of Lessons Explained. By Rev. W. G. Humphry, B.D. Fcap. 1s. 6d.

A Commentary on the Gospels for the Sundays and other Holy Days of the Christian Year. By Rev. W. Denton, A.M. New Edition. 3 vols. 8vo. 54s. Sold separately.

Commentary on the Epistles for the Sundays and other Holy Days of the Christian Year. By Rev. W. Denton, A.M. 2 vols. 36s. Sold separately.

Commentary on the Acts. By Rev. W. Denton, A.M. Vol. I. 8vo. 18s. Vol. II. 14s.

Notes on the Catechism. By Rev. A. Barry, D.D. 6th Edit. Fcap. 2s.

Catechetical Hints and Helps. By Rev. E. J. Boyce, M.A. 4th Edition, revised. Fcap. 2s. 6d.

Examination Papers on Religious Instruction. By Rev. E. J. Boyce. Sewed. 1s. 6d.

Church Teaching for the Church's Children. An Exposition of the Catechism. By the Rev. F. W. Harper. Sq. fcap. 2s.

The Winton Church Catechist. Questions and Answers on the Teaching of the Church Catechism. By the late Rev. J. S. B. Monsell, LL.D. 3rd Edition. Cloth, 3s.; or in Four Parts, sewed.

The Church Teacher's Manual of Christian Instruction. By Rev. M. F. Sadler. 21st Thousand. 2s. 6d.

Short Explanation of the Epistles and Gospels of the Christian Year, with Questions. Royal 32mo. 2s. 6d.; calf, 4s. 6d.

Butler's **Analogy of Religion**; with Introduction and Index by Rev. Dr. Steere. New Edition. Fcap. 3s. 6d.

——— **Three Sermons** on Human Nature, and Dissertation on Virtue. By W. Whewell, D.D. 4th Edition. Fcap. 8vo. 2s. 6d.

Lectures on the History of Moral Philosophy in England. By W. Whewell, D.D. Crown 8vo. 8s.
Kent's Commentary on International Law. By J. T. Abdy, LL.D. New and Cheap Edition. Crown 8vo. 10s. 6d.
A Manual of the Roman Civil Law. By G. Leapingwell, LL.D. 8vo. 12s.

FOREIGN CLASSICS.

A series for use in Schools, with English Notes, grammatical and explanatory, and renderings of difficult idiomatic expressions. Fcap. 8vo.

Schiller's Wallenstein. By Dr. A. Buchheim. 3rd Edit. 6s. 6d. Or the Lager and Piccolomini, 3s. 6d. Wallenstein's Tod, 3s. 6d.
—— Maid of Orleans. By Dr. W. Wagner. 3s. 6d.
—— Maria Stuart. By V. Kastner. 3s.
Goethe's Hermann and Dorothea. By E. Bell, M.A., and E. Wölfel. 2s. 6d.
German Ballads, from Uhland, Goethe, and Schiller. By C. L. Bielefeld. 3rd Edition. 3s. 6d.
Charles XII., par Voltaire. By L. Direy. 4th Edition. 3s. 6d.
Aventures de Télémaque, par Fénélon. By C. J. Delille. 2nd Edition. 4s. 6d.
Select Fables of La Fontaine. By F. E. A. Gasc. 14th Edition. 3s.
Picciola, by X. B. Saintine. By Dr. Dubuc. 11th Thousand. 3s. 6d.

FRENCH CLASS-BOOKS.

Twenty Lessons in French. With Vocabulary, giving the Pronunciation. By W. Brebner. Post 8vo. 4s.
French Grammar for Public Schools. By Rev. A. C. Clapin, M.A. Fcap. 8vo. 8th Edit. 2s. 6d.
French Primer. By Rev. A. C. Clapin, M.A. Fcap. 8vo. 4th Edit. 1s.
Primer of French Philology. By Rev. A. C. Clapin. Fcap. 8vo. 1s.
Le Nouveau Trésor; or, French Student's Companion. By M. E. S. 16th Edition. Fcap. 8vo. 3s. 6d.

F. E. A. GASC'S FRENCH COURSE.

First French Book. Fcap 8vo. 76th Thousand. 1s. 6d.
Second French Book. 37th Thousand. Fcap. 8vo. 2s. 6d.
Key to First and Second French Books. Fcap. 8vo. 3s. 6d.
French Fables for Beginners, in Prose, with Index. 14th Thousand. 12mo. 2s.
Select Fables of La Fontaine. New Edition. Fcap. 8vo. 3s.
Histoires Amusantes et Instructives. With Notes. 14th Thousand. Fcap. 8vo. 2s. 6d.

Practical Guide to Modern French Conversation. 12th Thousand. Fcap. 8vo. 2s. 6d.
French Poetry for the Young. With Notes. 4th Edition. Fcap. 8vo. 2s.
Materials for French Prose Composition; or, Selections from the best English Prose Writers. 15th Thousand. Fcap. 8vo. 4s. 6d. Key, 6s.
Prosateurs Contemporains. With Notes. 8vo. 6th Edition, revised. 5s.
Le Petit Compagnon; a French Talk-Book for Little Children. 10th Thousand. 16mo. 2s. 6d.
An Improved Modern Pocket Dictionary of the French and English Languages. 30th Thousand, with Additions. 16mo. Cloth. 4s. Also in 2 vols., in neat leatherette, 5s.
Modern French-English and English-French Dictionary. 2nd Edition, revised. In 1 vol. 12s. 6d. (formerly 2 vols. 25s.)

GOMBERT'S FRENCH DRAMA.

Being a Selection of the best Tragedies and Comedies of Molière, Racine, Corneille, and Voltaire. With Arguments and Notes by A. Gombert. New Edition, revised by F. E. A. Gasc. Fcap. 8vo. 1s. each; sewed, 6d.

CONTENTS.

MOLIERE:—Le Misanthrope. L'Avare. Le Bourgeois Gentilhomme. Le Tartuffe. Le Malade Imaginaire. Les Femmes Savantes. Les Fourberies de Scapin. Les Précieuses Ridicules. L'Ecole des Femmes. L'Ecole des Maris. Le Médecin malgré Lui.

RACINE:—Phèdre. Esther. Athalie. Iphigénie. Les Plaideurs. La Thébaïde; or, Les Frères Ennemis. Andromaque. Britannicus.

P. CORNEILLE:—Le Cid. Horace. Cinna. Polyeucte.

VOLTAIRE:—Zaïre.

GERMAN CLASS-BOOKS.

Materials for German Prose Composition. By Dr Buchheim. 7th Edition Fcap. 4s. 6d. Key, 3s.
A German Grammar for Public Schools. By the Rev. A. C. Clapin and F. Holl Müller. 2nd Edition. Fcap. 2s. 6d.
Kotzebue's Der Gefangene. With Notes by Dr. W. Stromberg. 1s.

ENGLISH CLASS-BOOKS.

A Brief History of the English Language. By Prof. Jas. Hadley, LL.D., of Yale College. Fcap. 8vo. 1s.
The Elements of the English Language. By E. Adams, Ph.D. 18th Edition. Post 8vo. 4s. 6d.
The Rudiments of English Grammar and Analysis. By E. Adams, Ph.D. 8th Edition. Fcap. 8vo. 2s.

By C. P. MASON, Fellow of Univ. Coll. London.

First Notions of Grammar for Young Learners. Fcap. 8vo. 10th Thousand. Cloth. 8d.
First Steps in English Grammar for Junior Classes. Demy 18mo. New Edition. 1s.

Outlines of English Grammar for the use of Junior Classes. 26th Thousand. Crown 8vo. 2s.

English Grammar, including the Principles of Grammatical Analysis. 24th Edition. 77th Thousand. Crown 8vo. 3s. 6d.

A Shorter English Grammar, with copious Exercises. 8th Thousand. Crown 8vo. 3s. 6d.

English Grammar Practice, being the Exercises separately. 1s.

Edited for Middle-Class Examinations.

With Notes on the Analysis and Parsing, and Explanatory Remarks.

Milton's Paradise Lost, Book I. With Life. 3rd Edit. Post 8vo. 2s.

—— Book II. With Life. 2nd Edit. Post 8vo. 2s.

—— Book III. With Life. Post 8vo. 2s.

Goldsmith's Deserted Village. With Life. Post 8vo. 1s. 6d.

Cowper's Task, Book II. With Life. Post 8vo. 2s.

Thomson's Spring. With Life. Post 8vo. 2s.

—— Winter. With Life. Post 8vo. 2s.

Practical Hints on Teaching. By Rev. J. Menet, M.A. 5th Edit. Crown 8vo. cloth, 2s. 6d.; paper, 2s.

Test Lessons in Dictation. 2nd Edition. Paper cover, 1s. 6d.

Questions for Examinations in English Literature. By Rev. W. W. Skeat, Prof. of Anglo-Saxon at Cambridge University. 2s. 6d.

Drawing Copies. By P. H. Delamotte. Oblong 8vo. 12s. Sold also in parts at 1s. each.

Poetry for the School-room. New Edition. Fcap. 8vo. 1s. 6d.

Geographical Text-Book; a Practical Geography. By M. E. S. 12mo. 2s.

The Blank Maps done up separately, 4to. 2s. coloured.

Loudon's (Mrs.) Entertaining Naturalist. New Edition. Revised by W. S. Dallas, F.L.S. 5s.

—— **Handbook of Botany.** New Edition, greatly enlarged by D. Wooster. Fcap. 2s. 6d.

The Botanist's Pocket-Book. With a copious Index. By W. R. Hayward. 3rd Edit. revised. Crown 8vo. Cloth limp. 4s. 6d.

Experimental Chemistry, founded on the Work of Dr. Stöckhardt. By C. W. Heaton. Post 8vo. 5s.

Double Entry Elucidated. By B. W. Foster. 12th Edit. 4to. 3s. 6d.

A New Manual of Book-keeping. By P. Crellin, Accountant. Crown 8vo. 3s. 6d.

Picture School-Books. In Simple Language, with numerous Illustrations. Royal 16mo.

School Primer. 6d.—School Reader. By J. Tilleard. 1s.—Poetry Book for Schools. 1s.—The Life of Joseph. 1s.—The Scripture Parables. By the Rev. J. E. Clarke. 1s.—The Scripture Miracles. By the Rev. J. E. Clarke. 1s.—The New Testament History. By the Rev. J. G. Wood, M.A. 1s.—The Old Testament History. By the Rev. J. G. Wood, M.A. 1s.—The Story of Bunyan's Pilgrim's Progress. 1s.—The Life of Christopher Columbus. By Sarah Crompton. 1s.—The Life of Martin Luther. By Sarah Crompton. 1s.

BOOKS FOR YOUNG READERS.
In 8 vols. Limp cloth, 6d. each.

The Cat and the Hen; Sam and his Dog Red-leg; Bob and Tom Lee; A Wreck——The New-born Lamb; Rosewood Box; Poor Fan; Wise Dog——The Three Monkeys——Story of a Cat, told by Herself——The Blind Boy; The Mute Girl; A New Tale of Babes in a Wood——The Day and the Knight; The New Bank-note; The Royal Visit; A King's Walk on a Winter's Day——Queen Bee and Busy Bee——Gull's Crag, a Story of the Sea.

First Book of Geography. By C. A. Johns. 1s.

BELL'S READING-BOOKS.
FOR SCHOOLS AND PAROCHIAL LIBRARIES.

The popularity which the 'Books for Young Readers' have attained is a sufficient proof that teachers and pupils alike approve of the use of interesting stories, with a simple plot in place of the dry combination of letters and syllables, making no impression on the mind, of which elementary reading-books generally consist.

The Publishers have therefore thought it advisable to extend the application of this principle to books adapted for more advanced readers.

Now Ready. Post 8vo. Strongly bound.

Masterman Ready. By Captain Marryat, R.N. 1s. 6d.
The Settlers in Canada. By Captain Marryat, R.N. 1s. 6d.
Parables from Nature. (Selected.) By Mrs. Gatty. 1s.
Friends in Fur and Feathers. By Gwynfryn. 1s.
Robinson Crusoe. 1s. 6d.
Andersen's Danish Tales. (Selected.) By E. Bell, M.A. 1s.
Southey's Life of Nelson. (Abridged.) 1s.
Grimm's German Tales. (Selected.) By E. Bell, M.A. 1s.
Life of the Duke of Wellington, with Maps and Plans. 1s.
Marie; or, Glimpses of Life in France. By A. R. Ellis. 1s.
Poetry for Boys. By D. Munro. 1s.
Edgeworth's Tales; a Selection. 1s.
Great Englishmen; Short Lives for Young Children. 1s.

Others in Preparation.

LONDON:
Printed by STRANGEWAYS & SONS, Tower Street, Upper St. Martin's Lane.

LaVergne, TN USA
20 October 2010
201513LV00002B/9/A